7 MISTAKES
WOMEN MAKE
THAT REPEL
GOOD MEN
And How To Reverse Them!

Joanna Hairabedian

Scripture references marked as "NKJV" are taken from the New King James Version®, Copyright © 1982 by Thomas Nelson. Used by permission. All rights reserved.

Scripture references marked "KJV" are taken from the King James Version in the Public Domain.

Scripture references marked "NIV" are taken from the Holy Bible, New International Version®, NIV® Copyright ©1973, 1978, 1984, 2011 by Biblica, Inc.® Used by permission. All rights reserved worldwide.

Scripture references marked "NLT" are taken from the Holy Bible, New Living Translation, copyright © 1996, 2004, 2015 by Tyndale House Foundation. Used by permission of Tyndale House Publishers, Inc., Carol Stream, Illinois 60188. All rights reserved.

Cover and Interior Layout @ 2024 Harvest Creek Publishing and Design
www.harvestcreek.net   email: info@harvestcreek.net

Ordering Information: Special discounts are available on quantity purchases by groups, churches, and other associations. For details, please contact the author at the information provided at the back of this book.

7 Mistakes Women Make That Repel Good Men—1st edition.

ISBN: 978-1-961641-11-2

Printed in The United States of America

CONTENTS

DEDICATION

*To the beautiful women of all ages reading this book on the journey of
love, inner transformation, and becoming the best version of you.
The best is yet to come!*

*To the incredible man of my dreams, my husband, Dr. David Hairabedian.
You are the wind under my wings and my #1 supporter.
Your love, support, wisdom, and insight helped me birth this book!*

*To my wonderful besties (you know who you are!)
and my family, prayer team, and friends for strengthening me
with your love, support, prayers, and encouragement.*

ACKNOWLEDGMENTS

Teamwork makes the dream work! I want to thank the following people who had a part in helping me shape the book:

- ♥ **Lindi Stoler,** as an amazing book and media strategist, your insights, book training, and incredible strategies for many of the book components helped bring my story to life. Without you, my book would not be what it's become. You're truly the best in the business!

- ♥ **Carron Hairabedian,** your sage wisdom and thoughtful notations, as you proofread the words on the pages, helped improve my writing.

- ♥ **Terry Johnston,** the years of business coaching and mentorship have inspired me to become a better version of myself, which has influenced the birthing of my first book.

- ♥ **Dr. Lee Benton,** for years as my TV Broadcast mentor and a powerful prayer warrior, you stood steadfast, believing with me for the man of my dreams until he finally arrived.

- ♥ **Koren Emerson,** you were one of the keys that helped unlock the love story for David and me. As a proofreader, your eagle eyes helped sharpen and fine-tune each sentence.

♥ **Sharon Murphin**, your honest feedback was invaluable. Your unwavering support and encouragement gave me the strength to complete the process.

♥ **Zenobia Smith**, my soul sister, your watchful eye, and protective heart during my courtship with David, helped us weave the love story we have today.

♥ **Kassel Row and Ralph Wood,** your photographic gifts beautifully immortalized my epic royal wedding day. The picture of David and me together in the Epilogue section speaks a thousand words.

♥ **Teresa Granberry**, you, and your team from Harvest Creek Publishing, did a fantastic job of combining all the components to create a beautiful and polished book.

♥ **Jackie McGirvin**, your editorial magic touch helped shape the flow of the book in the first round of editing.

♥ **Daniel Pham and Gabriela Ceron**, every woman needs her glam squad. Daniel, thank you for capturing the essence of the moment for my back cover photo. Gabriela, you did a beautiful job with my make-up.

PREFACE
A Note from the Author

My heart is excited about the journey you're about to embark on. Bringing positive change to someone's life is one of my greatest joys. With this book, you'll find guidance and hope for a meaningful connection with a good man.

In the United States, almost 50% of adults are single. Having been a divorce statistic myself, I, too, was navigating life solo, searching for love, and hoping to experience my *happily ever after.* My journey of being single spanned almost two decades.

As the author, I intimately understand the ache of waking up to an empty bed. I know what the longing for partnership with my divine soul mate feels like. I understand what it's like to be young and looking for your "Knight in Shining Armor." Having walked a parallel path in those shoes, I also understand the pain of rejection, abandonment, and betrayal from previous relationships with Mr. Wrong.

Life is a learning journey, and I became a student. In fact, I graduated from the University of "OUCH that Hurt! Now What?" Maybe you haven't attended that school, but you're single and want to find the right guy.

Being vulnerable with you, I've made every dating mistake in this book. Not realizing I was repelling the good men I sought. One day, in an ugly crying moment, I prayed for a spiritual mirror to be held up to my face. That brief prayer was a turning point, a catalyst that transformed my life.

The layers of self-discovery—the good, the bad, and the ugly unfolded. I embarked on a journey of learning to love myself. I started studying women who had successful relationships. What were they doing differently than me? What were the secrets to attracting and keeping a good man?

This book is more than words on paper; it's a guide, a source of insight, a mirror reflecting awareness. The lessons I've learned from my dating misadventures will benefit you greatly. Prepare to uncover the wisdom derived from my what-to-dos and what-not-to-dos. Uncover the secrets that enabled me to attract and hold on to the man I always desired. And yes, we are still happily married many years later. Do I practice what I preach? Yep.

I invite you to read my husband's note in the Epilogue. It's a testament to the authenticity of the journey you're about to embark on. The proof is in the results. Attracting Mr. Right is one thing, but keeping and maintaining a solid and joyful relationship is a unique challenge altogether.

This book is not about excusing bad behavior or blaming anyone. Each person is 100% responsible for their actions. Men and women are on two sides of the same coin, each accountable for their actions. This book is about creating awareness of our side of the coin, understanding relationship dynamics, and the roles we play.

My hope is to see you discover the keys to the love and happiness you deserve. What took me almost two decades to learn, you now hold at the tips of your fingers. If you commit to the journey, I promise you the romance results in your life will profoundly transform for the better. If I could do it, so can you!

In the next chapter, I share the pivotal moment when a spiritual mirror was held up to my face, sparking a journey of self-discovery and shocking insights.

As you turn the page, know you're not alone in your quest for love. You are not alone in the journey of transformation and creating awareness. The next chapter in your love story is waiting to be written. Let's write it together!

With heartfelt sincerity,

♥Joanna Hairabedian

INTRODUCTION

As you know, the quote above is an exaggeration, but sometimes it seems too true! Like most women, I dreamed of my mighty knight in shining armor who would ride in on his white horse and rescue me. He would be romantic, and we would have a special connection that only soulmates have. We would live happily ever after, just like in the movies. Did my first marriage play out like that? Ummm, not exactly. But keep reading!

Every woman wants her white knight, her defender. You deserve to have a guy who will honor, love, and cherish you, not one who will lie, cheat, and mistreat you. So why can it be challenging to find a good guy and have a forever happy ending?

The good news is you're going to learn what mistakes to avoid and how to attract and keep a good man for your happily ever after. Let's start with a few questions:

- ♥ Have you been rejected when the man you love says, "I'm sorry, but I don't love you anymore?"
- ♥ Do you wonder why the man you had a connection with suddenly disappeared?
- ♥ Is time running out on your biological clock?
- ♥ Has depression set in because you haven't yet found the right love connection?

♥ Are you a single mom or a successful career woman who can't seem to find "the one?"

♥ Do you believe all the good ones are taken?

♥ Do you feel judged when people ask, "Why are you still single?"

If you answered "Yes" to any of these questions, then you're at the right place, at the right time. Just like you, there was a time when I answered "Yes" to many of these questions.

I understand all too well the pain of rejection, betrayal, disappointment, unmet expectations, and those secret, ugly cry moments. Admittedly, I was a single woman for almost two decades—a woman rejected and betrayed by the man I loved. I was the divorcée, always looking for "Mr. Right." And I was a woman who made dating mistakes that repeatedly repelled good men. You already know that my alma mater is the University of OUCH That Hurt! where their slogan was, "Now how do I heal?"

Did I finally find Mr. Right and get my happily ever after? Yes. Are we still happily married many years later? Absolutely. And there is hope for you!

You are not alone; I want to affirm that you are strong and courageous. You are beautiful inside and out. You are worthy and deserve to have a superhero who will love, honor, and cherish you.

SUPERHERO DEACTIVATING WORDS AND BEHAVIORS

Do most of us women realize we do things and speak words that repel the very thing we want? Most of the time, we don't. I know I didn't.

We don't realize that our words and behaviors are what I call "**Superhero Deactivators,**" which will be addressed in detail in the ensuing chapters. As we journey together, I ask that you suspend your current perspectives and attitudes about men (and yourself) and be open-minded to new possibilities. Permit yourself to change your mind, given new information. Sometimes, it means letting go of something old to receive something new.

This book is not about dwelling on past hurts or blaming men for our pain; it's about empowering you to build a healthy, fulfilling relationship. You'll learn what mistakes to avoid and how to attract and keep a good guy for a lifetime of love!

Keep reading to learn the secret keys that will help unlock a whole new world for you. In gaining knowledge and understanding, you'll feel more confident and emanate a vibrant frequency to attract Mr. Right. Imagine as your energy shifts, attracting more fun because romantic opportunities have increased. Imagine feeling more secure because of your new skills to have a great relationship. And, most importantly, attracting a man who will love, honor, and cherish you.

Your future path lies in your willingness to examine your true, inner heart motivations honestly. This takes courage. I had to do it. Give yourself grace and compassion, and learn to forgive yourself. I promise you won't be sorry. Let's start at the beginning of the story.

WHEN MR. RIGHT BECOMES MR. WRONG

We all have the Ex who seemed to be the cat's meow, right? It was so sweet initially, but then the scratches came, sometimes turning into an infection that caused much pain.

Often, our man-picker is broken. Mine sure was. Back in my younger days, I met and fell in love with an ex (whom we'll call "Mr. Wrong"). Mr. Wrong may sound cliché, but I'm using terms like this for the purposes of teaching. I'll also be using the words Mr. Potential and Mr. Right.

My Mr. Wrong was successful, a leader in his community and church. He was charismatic, a good dancer, funny and intelligent. He seemed like a real superhero—my knight in shining armor. However, right after we tied the knot, it was like waking up with a completely different man.

On Day Two of what was supposed to be my happily ever after, Mr. Wrong began acting cold and distant. He was the opposite of how a newlywed should be. A sick feeling rose in my gut after a whole day of silent coldness. I couldn't take it anymore and finally confronted him in the bedroom.

As he stood beside the bed, getting ready to put on his shoes, I grabbed his arm and made him look me in the eyes. My heart raced as I asked him, "What's going on? Why are you acting so mean and distant?"

In a controlled, emotionless tone, Mr. Wrong looked me straight in the eyes and said, "I don't love you."

The silence seemed like an eternity as the words slowly registered. It felt like the blood drained out of my body, and shock hit me like a jolt of lightning. My ears couldn't believe what I'd just heard.

Dumbfounded, I stuttered, "WHAT? Whaa . . . whaa . . . what are you saying? What do you mean you DON'T LOVE me?"

He blankly stared at me.

In utter disbelief, I said, "Why would you push to marry me when I asked you about waiting?" The silence was unbearable.

Mr. Wrong finally answered, "I had doubts, but when I talked to our friends, they thought it was just fear."

Like a fish out of water, my mouth was gaping wide open as I stared at him. One hundred thoughts raced through my mind at the same time. He had talked to our friends, but not to me. Our friends had spoken to him, but not to me. Talk about a betrayal from those who were supposed to care about me.

Suddenly, I found myself in a dark twilight zone, which eventually plummeted into what felt like an emotional hell on earth. It turns out that he had a causal relationship with the truth and a well-disguised addiction to alcohol. Additionally, he was unaware of the meaning of "faithful" and had powerful desires for control, resulting in unpleasant and ugly actions towards me. *Yep, I could pick them.*

The ironic thing is when I looked into Mr. Wrong's eyes, I could see all the pain inside his soul, and my heart went out to him. He would drink because he tried to mask all the pain instead of dealing with it.

In those early hours of shocking new information, I fully committed to maintaining a heart of compassion. I wanted to make this work without considering the concept of divorce. Behind every addiction is the need for love, and I wanted to help him return to the man I first met.

I wanted to believe that deep down, a part of him was a good person and that he loved me. We had three separations during the next two years, all of which I initiated. It was a time when I felt my soul couldn't withstand his intentional, emotionally charged target practice. The separations were an attempt to establish boundaries from his ugly behavior patterns.

He would promise to change and agree to counseling if I returned home. Naturally, I would go back home thinking, "This time, it's going to work." Each time, for a few weeks, he acted attentive and affectionate, initiated time together, and spoke respectfully to me.

However, as the weeks passed, the counseling stopped, and the painful behaviors began again. After the third separation, tensions between us began to escalate. Mr. Wrong started blocking me from the bank accounts, forbidding me from going to church or from doing what I had done before we married.

Often, I'd wake up in the middle of the night with a feeling of terror, like something awful was going to happen. If I got up, I'd find the front door wide open, and Mr. Wrong was nowhere to be found. This was a routine that occurred several times a week and caused me to be fearful for my life.

I didn't know where he was or what he was doing. He didn't want me but didn't want to let me go. When he did talk to me, I was blamed for everything. He was a master at gaslighting. After we married, he also isolated me from friends and family. He didn't want me seeing or spending time with them.

So, how did I escape if he wasn't willing to let me go? There's a lot to be said for the power of prayer.

A WAY OF ESCAPE

One evening, we were at a restaurant, and I casually mentioned that I wanted to listen to Christian music after dinner. Mr. Wrong glared at me and then blew a gasket. The restaurant witnessed his roaring, "If you're going to desecrate our marriage like that, you can pack your bags and GET OUT!"

He thought I had nowhere to go, no friends, and would have to come crawling back for help. What he didn't know was that after the three previous separations and with him having left the door wide open on numerous nights, I finally got smart and began planning my exit.

I maintained my separate bank account (to which there was always money for savings), and we also had a joint account. I had quietly arranged to rent a room from a kind Jewish woman I met at a wedding. (Ironically, that wedding was one of my best friends who betrayed me with Mr. Wrong.)

When Mr. Wrong screamed at me to pack my bags and get out, I took a taxi back to the house. There, I packed everything that would fit in my car, left the house, and never looked back.

Again, the power of prayer helped steady my nerves and granted me courage in the dark nights of my soul. I moved out, but after a few weeks, he started harassing me with phone calls and threats again.

My mother was very concerned for my life. I would later find out that after the reception, she had caught a fleeting look of evil that flashed in Mr. Wrong's eyes when he looked at me in the elevator. The evil she saw gave her the shivers, and a feeling of dread overcame her.

As a result, when the harassment began after I left him, Mom whisked me to Europe for the summer to get away. I left the U.S. with a small suitcase and a carry-on bag. While there, an unexpected opportunity to attend a one-year TV production program in a local town presented itself, and I was accepted.

So, exactly how did my transformation journey unfold and eventually blossom? It all began on a cold, snowy night. I lay on the kitchen floor in my European studio like a broken rag doll, crying my eyes out. My divorce was final, and the dreams of a happily ever after were shattered.

After what seemed like an eternity of sobbing, I slowly raised my tear-stained face (complete with puffy, swollen eyes) and cried out to God, "How did this happen to me? How did I choose such a broken man? Please put up a mirror to my face and show me how I ended up in this mess!"

This moment of surrender and honesty marked the beginning of my transformation when a spiritual mirror was held up to my face.

It was the beginning of what would eventually lead me to write this book. A year later, I was back in the U.S., safe and free of Mr. Wrong. I had no desire to be called "Mrs." again, and becoming a (steadfast) nun seemed like a great idea!

In my sad eyes, all I could see was that men could not be trusted. To me, they were all liars, abusers, and cheaters. *Thankfully, I'd be wrong about that!* As my emotional healing journey unfolded, eventually, I was ready to explore love again, and I decided becoming a nun wasn't my true calling.

However, the unexpected happened. The clock ticked by year after year, and I was still a divorcée. Five years went by—no husband was in sight. Eight years passed—still single and dateless, with people asking, "Why don't you have a boyfriend yet?"

Eleven years went by. I was getting older, still single, and had no children. Depression set in as I researched having my eggs frozen. The cost was astronomical, so that was a no-go. Thirteen years went by—no man, no family of my own, no frozen eggs, no marriage.

There were great days when I stood in my truth and was strong and independent. Then there were the days when rejection, loneliness, and jealousy toward other women with good men would raise their ugly heads. *Lord, why not me? Why can't I share my life with a great husband? Why do I have to stay alone?*

In my journey of inner transformation, I learned valuable lessons that, if applied, can keep you from marrying your own Mr. Wrong. It will also help shorten the learning curve to attract Mr. Right and enhance your current relationship.

UNDERSTANDING IS THE BEGINNING OF KNOWLEDGE

First things first. If you haven't already done this, when presented with new information, now is the time to permit yourself to change your mind. It's easy to get stuck in an old mindset that isn't bringing you the results you desire in life. Go ahead and put your hand over your heart and say, "I give myself permission and grace to change my mind."

My journey to transformation and positive change began when I scraped myself off the kitchen floor, and a spiritual mirror was held up to my face. I recognized the need to take personal responsibility and break free from the blame game.

After committing myself to a better understanding, I learned what caused me to make my choices. Our current culture breeds an entitled, narcissistic victim mentality.

Initially, that was me. I blamed God, Mr. Wrong, and the people who abandoned me. I blamed my friends who betrayed me and the world because of the pain of marrying Mr. Wrong. It was all about *my* pain, *my* feelings, *my* victimhood. Yes, I needed to heal, but it couldn't happen until I left my pity party.

> *You are accountable for your actions, your decisions, your life;*
> *no one else but you.*
> CATHERINE PULSIFER, YOUR POSITIVE OASIS

After much frustration and tears, I realized the importance of understanding how I attracted and married a man like Mr. Wrong—someone who was the exact opposite of what I wanted. Next, I had to evaluate why I allowed someone to pressure me into marriage. And finally, I had to accept responsibility for my mistakes in the marriage regardless of his behavior. This book will delve into every aspect of this.

Understanding my part in the failure of the marriage didn't excuse his actions.

It would have been easy to play the victim, blaming Mr. Wrong and not understanding how I found myself in a marriage spawned in hell. Without learning from my mistakes, I would have most likely spun in the same wash, rinse, and repeat cycles with two, three, or even four divorces.

**If you aren't getting the desired outcomes,
it's time to evaluate and make changes.**

Are you sick and tired of your outcomes? Here are some questions to ponder:

- ♥ Have you ever sat down and thought about how you are with men?
- ♥ What do you really feel about them?
- ♥ What are your heart's attitudes toward them?
- ♥ What words do you use?
- ♥ What kinds of topics do you talk about in general?
- ♥ Have you analyzed your past relationship, dating experiences, and those undesirable outcomes?
- ♥ What could you have done differently?
- ♥ Are you aware of the expressions on your face?

For example, I unknowingly walked around with a frown until someone stopped me and asked why I was angry. I didn't realize that my face was reflecting the negative thoughts circulating in my head which appeared as anger to others. The impression I was giving men was that I was unapproachable. More to come on this.

As my awareness increased, it became apparent that certain behaviors, mindsets, and communications kept me stuck inside the singles' circle. Over time, I started reflecting on what women who have a good relationship with a great guy were doing. I would talk to these women, study them, and learn from their behaviors.

- ♥ What was it about their behavior that attracted good men?
- ♥ What were their mannerisms?
- ♥ What specific words did they use?
- ♥ Were they emanating a particular energy?

The more my self-awareness grew, and the more I evaluated my past attitudes, responses, and mindsets, the more I could spot other women making the same mistakes as I used to. Ultimately, it became apparent to me that women as a collective whole were making similar "man mistakes" or superhero deactivator behaviors. This was a significant revelation.

> **Imagine attracting Mr. Right and enjoying happily ever after.**
> **Imagine being free and having joy.**
> **Imagine having a better connection with men.**
> **And if you're married, imagine having a better marriage.**

My husband, David, and I initially met through a mutual friend, who introduced us for a possible business connection and nothing more. In that season of my life, I was very content. I loved and honored myself and was not looking for a husband because I had healthy self-esteem and a strong spiritual relationship with my Creator.

David sent me a social media friend request at our friend's suggestion. But when I checked out his profile, I ignored his request, thinking he might be a bit of a project! A year later, I received a call from David's friend, inviting me to have dinner with them because David was in town.

It's intriguing that there was no initial spark between David and me when we first met. I did not know this was my future husband. We each thought the other was great, but there was no spark. We had a lively conversation, a wonderful dinner, and a fabulous evening, but that was it.

David had a life-transforming ministry (which he still has today) called Heart of America Prison Ministry. It provides beautiful discipleship bibles to a waiting list of inmates wanting to change their lives.

A couple of weeks after our initial dinner meeting, I felt inclined to donate to David's ministry. He called me back to thank me for the donation, not realizing it was the same woman he had met at dinner two weeks prior. Over the ensuing year, we became good friends and prayer partners and worked on various projects together.

A year after we met, David was invited back to California for some speaking engagements. He knew about my musical gift and asked me to sing at one of his events.

When I entered the venue, our eyes connected, and we instantly felt a mutual spark. It was like someone lifted off an invisible veil. At first, we both tried to hide our attraction for each other.

But once we talked about our mutual attraction, we agreed to enter a committed relationship and assess if we were meant to be married. We took it one step at a time and decided that we would remain good friends even if we weren't a marriage match.

Our love story is beautiful, and we waited until our wedding night to consummate our union. Countless people refer to us as the "dynamic duo" and the "perfect puzzle piece match" for each other.

Imagine the outcome if I hadn't humbled myself to ask God to show me my mistakes. Imagine if I hadn't been willing to change. I would have missed my happily ever after entirely. I'd still be in the singles circle, or worse yet, in another cycle of bad partnership.

> **It takes courage to lean in, admit the good, bad, and ugly about yourself, and accept/forgive yourself.**

Walking into the unknown of change requires courage. It's a choice to say "No" to fear and "Yes" to courage and take the steps it takes to do it. *You can do this.*

> *There is beauty in the unknown and beauty in what may be,*
> *beauty in the promises of tomorrow,*
> *and beauty in all we cannot yet see.*
> ERIN FORBES, FIRE AND ICE: THE EMBER SWORD

Are you ready to get started? If so, I've got you. You can apply the principles discussed within these pages, whether you're single, divorced, widowed, looking for the right guy, or simply hoping to improve your marriage.

Together, we will uncover the mistakes that have been hindering your romance results and the blessings in your life. In the next chapter, we will look at one of the top mindsets that repels good men and can sour a good relationship.

The great news is you're going to learn how to reverse this. Never give up! Say "Yes" to you. Say "Yes" to a wonderful man waiting for you. Accept your forever happiness!

Chapter One

THE WIIFM SYNDROME
(What's In It for Me?)

All joking aside, doesn't it seem like people are more self-centered, entitled, and operate from a victim mentality? Do you seem to meet more takers than givers? Does your friend consistently have a crisis that needs fixing, but when you need something, they're unavailable? Or perhaps you are that friend. Have you ever found yourself cornered by a chatterbox who won't stop talking or complaining?

The common denominator in these questions is what I call "**The WIIFM Syndrome,**" which stands for "*What's In It For Me?*" Yep. It's all about me, me, me, me, me, me, me!

Before we examine the actual mistakes women make in relationships, we have two specific topics to discuss. These comprise the core foundation of all the other mistakes and are vital to understanding. This chapter covers the first topic: *WIIFM.*

As we've already discussed, it takes courage and humility to examine ourselves honestly and recognize both the good and the not-so-good aspects of our personalities. CONGRATULATIONS! You are doing it—which sets you apart from other women. So, let's begin.

In this self-exploration, I reiterate the difference between addressing past hurts and focusing on your personal growth. While healing from past painful experiences is necessary, this book primarily aims at helping us recognize our own hearts, attitudes, and mindsets that possibly limit our romantic opportunities. We also need to acknowledge the things that sour a good relationship. So, let's talk about the *What's In It For Me?* mindset.

There are two forms of *WIIFM* attitudes. The healthy *WIIFM* mentality helps you do good business, maintain appropriate boundaries, and have a balanced give-and-take in relationships. The unhealthy form of *WIIFM* revolves around an unhealthy sense of entitlement. Thinking that others should serve and cater to your needs is a self-centered expectation. It's not based on a healthy mindset of equal give and take. The heart's focus is all about yourself and how others should fulfill your dreams, rescue you, help you financially, complete you, etc. Essentially, these inner motivations played a part in why I wanted to get married.

7 Mistakes explores the unhealthy form of *WIIFM* which is typically rooted in a self-centered and selfish mindset that repels good men and taints what started as a good relationship. Unhealthy *WIIFM* caused me and countless other women to marry Mr. Wrong.

Most of the time, we don't realize how selfish we are, which leads to painful roads like it did for me. I wish I'd paid attention to this quote, which many consider to be the gold standard by which to gage ourselves:

> *Love is patient. Love is kind. It does not envy, it does not boast, it is not proud. It does not dishonor others, it is not self-seeking, it is not easily angered, it keeps no record of wrongs. Love does not delight in evil but rejoices with the truth.*
> *It always protects, always trusts, always hopes, always perseveres.*
> 1 CORINTHIANS 13:4-7, NIV

As we explore the unhealthy *WIIFM* it's important to examine how our culture contributes to this mindset through media. How often do we read magazine articles about "*getting the man*" to care for **you**? Many articles are written on how to get him to buy **you** things and get what **you** can get out of him. Some music videos depict women as seductresses who use their bodies to gain material things and power over men. It's all about "**what you can do for me.**"

> **Media stereotypes of men and women**
> **play into unsuccessful relationships.**

Let me ask: How many television shows teach women to grow in their identity as royalty from the inside out instead of being conditioned to use sex as a tool for control and manipulation? How many songs teach girls to be prostitutes and sex slaves instead of honoring and respecting their bodies? How many rap songs teach boys to hate women, calling them "hoes" and "bitches?"

MY BARBIE STORY

From a young age, Barbie dolls, TV shows, and movies expose us to messaging that depict women as man-stealers, victims in need of rescue, controlling nitpickers, or seductresses. For example, when I was a little girl, one game I loved to play was Barbie and Ken. What you're about to read is a classic example of media programming. My Barbie adventures would go something like this:

> *Once upon a time, there was Good Barbie. She was beautiful, with long, flowing hair and blue-green eyes. She was sweet, fun, and athletic. One day, Good Barbie met Ken doll; he was tall, dark, and handsome. Ken was also strong, wealthy, and athletic.*
>
> *They had a wonderful time together until Bad Barbie came along their way. Bad Barbie was also beautiful and charming with long, red, flowing hair. She became friends with Ken and Good Barbie, but Bad Barbie secretly liked Ken.*
>
> *Bad Barbie plotted to steal Ken's attention, so she set up Good Barbie to make it look like she was doing bad things. That way, Ken wouldn't like her anymore.*

Naturally, Ken started to like Bad Barbie, not knowing she was really the bad one. Bad Barbie decided that Good Barbie needed to disappear, so she hired kidnappers. Magically, Ken found out the truth and rescued Good Barbie. They got married and lived happily ever after.

Truth be told, when I married Mr. Wrong, I thought we would live happily ever after, just like my childhood Barbie story. As children, there is an expectation instilled in us to believe that "happily ever after" just magically happens. We feel we need someone to rescue us. How often do you hear a friend say, "I just want a man to take care of me?"

Therefore, it's important to take a quick look at how media stereotypes fuel our mindsets, creating unrealistic expectations and false beliefs about relationships. As women, we complain men don't know how to communicate, are detached from their feelings, and don't know how to be vulnerable.

What I'm about to share next is quite thought-provoking. On the following page are some of the most common media stereotypes of men and women in the table below. As you read the stereotypes, keep the following questions in mind:

- ♥ Do you see your identity connected to any of these stereotypes?
- ♥ Are any of your perspectives about men identifiable with some of these stereotypes?
- ♥ Have any of these stereotypes played a part in your relationship's failure because of unrealistic or unmet expectations?
- ♥ Have any of these stereotypes made you feel pressured to conform and change yourself to attract a man?

STEREOTYPE ROLES OF A MAN	STEREOTYPE ROLES OF A WOMAN
The Fairytale Prince He's the perfect, handsome rescuer who rides in on a white horse. He rescues the princess, and they live happily ever after.	**The Fairytale Princess** She's the perfect, beautiful maiden waiting for her prince to sweep her off her feet. They fall in love and live happily ever after.
The Bumbling Husband He is clueless and inept. The Bumbling Husband cannot handle household tasks, and his wife dominates him. He's the "Yes, dear" man.	**The Damsel in Distress** She is helpless and one who needs to be rescued. She's in some danger, financial trouble, or requires help in some other way. The Damsel needs a man to take care of her.
The "Bad Boy" Alpha-Male He is ultra-dominant and controlling—the sexy bad boy, dressed in black, who rides in on a motorcycle and sweeps women off their feet.	**The Seductress** She is seductive and manipulative to control men. This reduces her to an object of desire based on her looks. She steals another woman's husband.
The "Nice Guy" He is passive—a nice guy who always finishes last and never gets the girl.	**The Nagging Wife/Girlfriend** She complains, is critical, and is hard to please.
The Pushover He is passive, weak, easily controlled, and manipulated by women.	**The Career-Obsessed Woman** She is cold, childless, heartless, and ruthless.
The Business Tycoon He is the narcissistic multi-millionaire who will step on anyone and anything to get his way. He's a seducer of women.	**The Weak Woman** She is excessively emotional, needy, and irrational.

These stereotypes influence both men and women in how they view themselves and how their partners perceive them. These stereotypes ultimately affect how men and women relate to and interact in a relationship with each other.

The most recent Barbie movie is a case in point. What were some of the movie's key messages? Women don't like men, and men don't like women. The Barbies are happy and living life to the fullest; the Kens go unnoticed and are just existing. Notice the subtle messaging in this?

> **It's important to understand how these stereotypes play into relationship failures and what repels good men.**

Comedians often use emasculating humor to mock men for their perceived weaknesses or emotional vulnerability. It promotes harmful stereotypes and discourages men from being authentic with their feelings. Hmmm . . . why aren't men more vulnerable?

On the flip side, other portrayals of the alpha male may focus on hyper-masculinity and dominance. This can then foster an unhealthy and unrealistic expectation for men to conform to aggressive and controlling behaviors.

Then you have stereotypes of a beta male often depicted as a passive, sensitive, and less dominant man. The beta man is a woman's "best friend" and treats her nicely and lovingly, but he's not the guy she's attracted to. However, the powerful alpha male, aka the bad boy who abuses her, is the one she wants. How often have you heard a friend, or you say, "I'm attracted to bad boys?"

In researching this book, I interviewed men about their perspectives on the mistakes women make. It's been eye-opening to hear their stories and experiences. These are nice, good men. For example, one man was 45 years old and told me women consistently rejected him because he was "too nice." Even though he's good-looking and successful, women aren't attracted to him.

Another young man I interviewed was 23 years old. He shared that he likes and prefers women. However, his experience with women has been that they don't accept him for who he is; they criticize him and then reject him because, again, he's too nice! So, he's currently with a guy because it is easier and drama-free.

Can you see how the media stereotypes influence an unhealthy mindset for a woman to choose the "bad boy" who brings her heartbreak instead of the "nice guy" who loves and respects her? *Nice guys finish last.* Not only that, but many women unknowingly damage his self-esteem. We will discuss this further in Chapter Three.

Initially, I expected that my Mr. Potential would meet all my needs, rescue me, and help make all my dreams come true. Meeting Mr. Wrong seemed like the answer to my prayers for a husband. Hey, I had found a good guy who would help make **my** dreams come true, take care of **me,** and help **me** with **my** music plans, etc.

We were moving quickly and dated for just over six months when Mr. Wrong proposed. He respected and agreed with my values of not sleeping with each other before marriage. We were also getting pastoral marriage counseling and doing everything *the right way.*

As the wedding date quickly approached, I felt uneasy and didn't know why. The pastor counseling us said feelings of conflict were normal and encouraged us to keep going as planned. The closer we got to the wedding day, the more distant Mr. Wrong became. I talked with him about postponing the wedding and giving ourselves more time to walk things out. He was very adamant about getting married and assured me he wanted us to spend the rest of our lives together.

What stopped me from pausing the wedding? Part of me loved the fact that I was going to be a bride and have a husband. I wanted a life partner to complete me. My subconscious mindset was about what he would do for me, not how we could serve each other.

Conversely, I was torn and constantly prayed for a "sign" showing I shouldn't marry Mr. Wrong. Something interesting happened while I sought a sign from God to dissuade me from going ahead with this life-altering choice. Two distinct friends of mine, who were unacquainted with one another, had an identical dream. In their dream, I was murdered after getting married. Thankfully, their dreams were only a metaphor!

Thinking they were doing the right thing, they each went separately to the pastor counseling Mr. Wrong and myself. They each told the pastor about their dreams instead of coming directly to me. He instructed them not to say anything to me. They trusted his judgment as a pastor, and so they kept silent!

The pastor also kept silent and never told me about the dreams—knowing I was feeling conflicted about getting married. Had he told me about the dreams, I would have seen that as my warning not to marry Mr. Wrong.

As I shared in the Introduction, the second day after we were married, Mr. Wrong told me he didn't love me and behaved like a completely different man from that point on. As you know, everything escalated from there. On a side note: Often, we don't realize that rejection can be God's protection.

> **Sometimes, our viewpoint about rejection needs a mindset shift. Even though rejection can be excruciatingly painful, choose a different perspective. View it as something that may have protected you from a guy who's not good for you!**

Have people ever betrayed, abandoned, or rejected you? Have you ever had someone tell you they don't love you anymore and walk away?

It would have been easy to blame Mr. Wrong for all the pain, trauma, and hurt he caused me. However, deep down, I knew I had to humble myself and take responsibility for my part. I knew that if I didn't make changes within myself, I'd most likely repeat the same mistake with a different face in a different place.

> **There are times when moments are pivotal in one direction or another in a relationship.**

I made two "moment" mistakes and learned from each of them. As I healed in those areas, it was easy to spot other women who were making the same mistakes.

For example, when I came back home from the first separation, Mr. Wrong was initially trying to change and was being thoughtful and attentive. Unfortunately, I was unaware of the critical impasse we had reached and was consumed by my pain.

One mistake was highlighting things he needed to change and how he should be doing that. It was because, deep down, I hadn't forgiven him and was still angry. It was a passive/aggressive way to get back at him.

For instance, I told him he needed to lose weight and go to the gym. What prompted me to say this? It wasn't about his health. No, he had painfully nitpicked my body, including pressuring me to get a breast job. So I simply wanted to dish it back at him since nothing about me was acceptable to him. He had developed a significant pot belly, and I wanted him to slim down because I have a distaste for pot bellies. Sarcastically, I referred to him as the Pillsbury doughboy, poking his stomach and recreating the familiar sound from the commercial. (Oh, and incidentally, I did not get the breast job!).

Another mistake was my constant complaining about the way he did things. Initially, he attempted to change, but my complaints caused him to doubt his ability to do it correctly. His mental balloon was deflated.

When a guy feels like he can't win, he'll stop trying.

At that time, I struggled with unforgiveness and felt justified in my pain. I would consistently bring up his past behaviors that had hurt me. However, it's a form of revenge. My behavior resembled an ice pick piercing thin ice.

Over time, I walked through my journey of healing. The process included letting go of the guilt for allowing myself to be pressured and making a bad choice, forgiving myself for the mistakes I made, and forgiving Mr. Wrong. Forgiveness is a *powerful* thing, and it allows freedom to fill your soul. It never excuses what someone else did. It allows you to escape the hook of darkness. Do you need to forgive yourself? Do you need to let go of guilt or condemnation?

Awareness is the key to a breakthrough.

Are you aware of the most unlikely teachers who have crossed your path? Throughout my period of being single, I discovered valuable lessons from the men I went out with. Who would have thought? As my personal awareness and self-analysis abilities grew, the men I met on the journey were some of my best teachers.

For example, I met a nice guy at the gym who was attractive, fit, and attentive. We would banter back and forth, and it became apparent he was attracted to me. And ultimately, he invited me to dinner at a nice restaurant.

During dinner, I talked almost the entire time about myself, complained about everything, and discussed the world's woes. I didn't ask him any questions about himself or give him a chance to speak. It goes without saying that we never went on another date after that.

After our date, it was obvious I had repelled him because he cooled off when we saw each other at the gym. After analyzing my date based on his distancing, I had the courage to ask him for input. He hesitated, not sure what he should say, but was honest with me and said, "Joanna, you're a great person, but you complain about everything, and it's all about you." *Can someone say, "OUCH!"*

As painful and embarrassing as it was to hear his words, it made me stop and think about what he said. Essentially, I had ignored him, didn't care to know about him, and was self-absorbed about myself. He was right! And to this day, I'm thankful he dared to tell me the truth. I was grateful for my ability to maturely listen, analyze, and honestly examine what needed to be changed.

From that point forward, I decided that someone's experience with me would leave them feeling blessed or encouraged in some way.

> **The critical components of the *WIIFM Syndrome* are: selfishness, complaining, and self-centeredness.**

Does like attract like? Do selfish people attract selfish people? Does a generous person with healthy boundaries attract another generous person with healthy boundaries? As I became conscious of the changes I needed, I realized there were many others thinking like my old *WIIFM* mindset.

ALL I WANT IS A MAN

For instance, I had met a woman named Sylvia. She was tall and beautiful, with a model's facial bone structure, bubbly, fun, witty, and a successful saleswoman. Heads would turn when she walked into a room, yet she'd never been married and desperately wanted to be in a relationship.

I couldn't figure out how she was still single until we were at lunch one day. Sylvia was talking about how she would meet these guys who seemed great. But then she would discover they were either married, commitment-phobes, or guys who eventually just disappeared. Sound familiar?

In a practical tone, she told me, "Ya know, Joanna, I love my job, and I make incredible money, but I just want a husband who will take care of *me!* I can have the babies, and he can bring home the bacon and buy *me* beautiful things."

As those words rang in my ears, it suddenly hit me like a ton of bricks as to why she was still single. She had the *WIIFM Syndrome.* Her motives for wanting a husband were selfish. It reminded me of my selfish motives before marrying Mr. Wrong.

Her mindset wasn't based on how she could complement his life and how they could be better together. It was a selfish mentality based on wanting someone else to take care of her financially. As successful as she was, she didn't want to pay her own bills or manage responsibility. It was all about *WIIFM* and what *he* was going to do for *her*!

THE CACKLING HENS

One evening, David (my current husband) and I were having dinner at a very elegant restaurant. The soft glow of the flickering candlelight highlighted the sparkles of the crystal chandeliers. Romantic music played in the background. The ambiance resembled a movie scene until two couples came in and seated themselves at the table directly across from us.

There was only a 2-ft aisle that separated our tables. It was apparent that both couples had been married for a long time, were excellent friends, and their kids were growing up together. Because of the proximity of their table, we could hear every word.

Usually, you can tune out other people's conversations, but not in this case. The two wives dominated the couple's conversation and sounded like cackling hens who wouldn't stop talking and complaining about everything. It was unbelievable. They talked about themselves, other friends' personal matters, their children, their friend's children's behavior, and the list went on.

The pitch of their voices grated even my ears. My husband and I glanced over at their table several times. We felt so sorry for these men who had to go home with these women. We watched the poor husbands just sitting there with pained, polite expressions on their faces.

Occasionally, the husbands would try to inject a comment, only to be talked over and dismissed by their wives. Can you say dishonoring AND disrespectful? Both men were attractive and seemed very kind and polite despite the wives' self-centered behavior. It was sad to observe how they just sat at the table with glazed expressions, unacknowledged, disregarded, and unheard during the entire dinner. You could tell the husbands were used to this kind of behavior from their wives.

Did these women realize the mistakes they were making by dominating the conversation and disregarding their husband's feelings? Do you think the husbands felt dishonored by their wives' self-centered dinner talk? Is this the behavior of a woman that unknowingly drives a man to seek attention elsewhere? Would you be surprised to hear the man say, "I don't love you anymore" after going through years of the example above?

According to the National Institute of Health's research, the top three causes of divorce are:

- ♥ Lack of commitment (this is #1).
- ♥ Too much arguing and conflict (promotes lack of intimacy).
- ♥ Infidelity.

As my husband David says, "Little keys unlock big doors and big doors swing on small hinges." How we do *anything* is how we do *everything*.

The women in this example represented the epitome of *WIIFM*. Instead of making an intention to include their husbands in the conversation, they did the opposite. They were focused on what *they* had to say, what *they* thought was important, and what *they* thought should be the topic of the conversation, completely dishonoring their husbands by ignoring them.

What if it had been the reverse situation, with the husbands ignoring them? Can you imagine if these women were on a date with a good Mr. Potential and operated in this type of *WIIFM* Attitude (just like I used to do)? Wouldn't this make the guy feel unimportant, dismissed, and unheard? What healthy man is going to be attracted to that kind of behavior? He's going to be repelled by it.

How often are we doing this to others in life and not just the men? In my travels, I've met countless women who had been married for 12 years, 17 years, 20 years, etc., whose husbands have said, "I don't love you anymore and want a divorce."

When a woman is unknowingly engaging in any form of these superhero deactivator behaviors (like the two women at dinner), you can see how a man might tell his wife of 15 years, "I don't love you anymore." To her, it might seem out of the blue. But from his perspective, he's been continuously ignored, unappreciated, made to feel like a nobody, unheard, and expected to help with household duties. To top it off, nothing he does is right.

> *It's better to live alone in the desert*
> *than with a quarrelsome, complaining wife.*
> PROVERBS 21:19 NLT

Naturally, there are two sides to every coin. But, right now, we are looking at our side of the coin as women and examining our own behaviors. Remember, it is a good thing as you begin to recognize *WIIFM* Behaviors! The important thing is to learn and understand *why* you made the choices you have. What is at the root? It's important to forgive yourself without condemnation, guilt, or shame but with grace.

CHOOSING A DIFFERENT RESPONSE LEADS TO A DIFFERENT RESULT

During my healing journey, I discovered a crucial realization about men: **Every good man has an inherent desire to be a superhero.** Sometimes, they don't know how to be a superhero. At other times, women engaged in behaviors that deactivated the inner superhero in the man.

Women don't realize how these superhero deactivators or what I call "man-breaker" behaviors repel a good man and sour a good relationship. We'll go into detail on man-breaking behaviors in the next chapter. Throughout our lives, every woman has played (or is playing) the role of a superhero deactivator in some way and isn't aware of it. That was me.

At other times, women can intentionally engage in superhero deactivators because a man or something in the past hurt her, and she won't allow healing in her soul. Typically, soul wounds are the root in these WIIFM behaviors.

THE CLUELESS TALKER

I was at dinner with a business associate. Annette was very attractive with a successful commercial real estate business. She was a foody with excellent taste in life, but she'd been single for a long time after a divorce and was in search of her soul mate.

Knowing my associate wanted to meet a good man, I invited my friend, Joshua, to join us. He was a successful businessman; he was handsome, a foody, generous, smart, and an exceptional dresser. I asked both to dinner because I felt there might be a spark of some kind toward each other.

Dinner was very interesting, to say the least. I had never seen my associate with a man she was interested in. She differed greatly from the calm, cool, and collected woman I knew. Joshua asked her engaging questions because he wanted to know more about who she was. She became animated, trying to be cute, funny, and knowledgeable. She went into detail about her answers and talked all about herself, her successes, her opinions, and all her accolades. My friend thought these things would impress him.

However, when he would say something in response to her answers, she would cut him off and interrupt him. Then, she would go into a long dissertation on her opinion. She asked him *one* question about himself but then didn't engage him in the conversation he was trying to have with her. She was focused on what she had to say—*WIIFM.*

She was obviously interested in him and casually asked him to have dinner at a great restaurant that she loved. He was very gracious but did not take her up on the dinner invitation or ask for her number.

Several things transpired in this situation. First, Annette did most of the talking, and he did most of the listening to her talk, talk, talk. Second, she didn't ask questions about him, his life, his work, etc. Next, she constantly interrupted him to give her opinion, cutting him off and not allowing him to finish his thoughts.

2

And finally, she asked him out instead of allowing him to invite her, and because she repelled him, she was rejected.

On a side note: Instead of asking him out, she could have given him the opportunity to ask her out by talking about some restaurants she heard were fabulous and how she would like to visit. This approach would have given him an opening to ask her out (if he was interested). Instead, not only did she repel him, but she was also rejected.

> **The good guys often need an opening to take action in asking you out.**

If a guy doesn't know you that well, you can talk about activities you like, such as trying new restaurants, going to the movies, sports games, etc. This gives him ideas on what kind of date he can ask you out for. Doing this will provide him with a win by removing his fear of rejection and boosting his confidence.

My work associate was presented with the possibility of a love connection with a good man. She blew it by making mistakes that repelled him. Guess what? She's still single because she's not coachable and refuses to look at herself.

Are you coachable? Are you willing to look honestly at what you're doing/not doing? It speaks volumes when someone is unwilling to make changes to obtain better results. It tells me they may not be ready for a relationship with a good man. Most likely, there are unhealed hurts and fears they subconsciously don't want to face. As a result, you hear the excuse, "I just can't seem to find the right guy! The mantra "All the good ones are taken" is supported by your "Yes" friends.

Where are you at in your relationship journey? Are you dominating conversations? Are you interrupting people before they finish their sentences? What are your inner motivations for wanting a marriage partner? Are you willing to make changes within yourself? Do you *need* someone to take care of you, provide for you, promote you, and make you complete? Is there a deeper, hidden fear of love that acts as a protection mechanism?

> *Seek first the kingdom of God . . .*
> *and all these things will be added unto you.*
> MATTHEW 6:33 NKJV

In other words, seek the good *WIIFM* (putting others first) and not the bad *WIIFM* (selfishness).

SUMMARIZING THIS CHAPTER

There are three primary lessons I learned from these personal experiences and from those around me.

♥ Lesson #1

It is in the honest examination that we come to an awareness of the deeper motives of our hearts for wanting to get married. When I was able to adjust my mindset about why I wanted a marriage and life partner, it went from a *WIIFM* mindset to that of "How can I honor what's important to HIM?" My heart's intention and attitude became, "How can I make HIS life better for knowing me?" Then, I would attract a man who had the same principle.

> **As a form of consistent practice, I applied the mindset of "What can I do to encourage, support or listen to someone else?"**

♥ Lesson #2

I had to learn how to talk less, listen more, and engage a person in conversation. I had to learn how to talk about positive things, not negative and morbid things. There's a reason we were born with two ears and one mouth. Learning to listen with both ears took a lot of practice for me. I became intentional about learning how to ask other people about their interests, hobbies, wins, and losses in life. I aimed to find out what was important to them, listen with my two ears, and talk with my one mouth in proper proportion.

♥ **Lesson #3**

I practiced courageous change and humbled myself to acknowledge my negative behaviors. I took personal responsibility and learned to identify my selfish or annoying inner motivations and change them.

My husband David and I have been happily married for many years. Are things perfect? No, there's always room to grow as individuals and couples. However, had I not learned from the above lessons and made changes within myself, I'd never have attracted a wonderful man like David. He also has a servant's heart and is generous and supportive. I attracted and recognized a man with a servant's heart because I now had a servant's heart.

HOMEWORK ASSIGNMENT:

Now it's time to get honest with yourself. Please answer the following questions. Remember: The truth sets you free.

♥ If single (or married), what are/were your deeper motivations to get married? What emotional, financial, biological, and spiritual needs do/did you think being married would fulfill? Is/Was there a deeper *WIIFM* root?

_____

_____

_____

_____

_____

_____

_____

_____

_____

_____

♥ List three adjectives (words only) that come to you when you see the word "Love." **Don't think about it; just write the first three words that come to mind**. Think about what came to mind for you. i.e., disappointment, anger, distrust, joy, fulfillment, etc. This exercise helps create an awareness of some inner feelings.

_____

_____

_____

♥ Based on what you read in this chapter, what three things come to mind that you may do that repel good men?

_____

_____

_____

_____

_____

_____

_____

_____

PRACTICAL APPLICATION EXERCISES

This week, ask someone (friend, new acquaintance, co-worker, etc.) out to lunch or coffee. Make it your intention to support them in some fashion. For example, ask them to share an experience that was life-changing for them (it can be anything). **Listen and don't give your opinion.**

♥ When appropriate, affirm and validate the thoughts and truths they share. Conclude the lunch by offering a kind affirmation or positive encouragement. The goal is to make them feel blessed and heard. The purpose of the exercise is to create an awareness of how to make your man feel heard and blessed.

♥ Date of the lunch: _____

♥ Journal your lunch experience below, reflecting on the following:

    o   How many times did you want to interrupt that person?

    o   What was their story?

    o   How did it feel to sit and focus on them while they were sharing?

    o   Did you find your mind trying to wonder?

    o   How did they feel after this encounter with you?

    o   Was there anything else you noticed?

_____

_____

_____

_____

_____

_____

_____

_____

_____

_____

_____

_____

♥ Perform three random acts of kindness. Document your experience, listing the thoughts that crossed your mind while demonstrating kindness. Was there an "*Aha!*" moment for you? If so, what was it?

_____

_____

_____

_____

_____

_____

_____

_____

_____

♥ What three things did you do? What happened with each encounter? Describe the emotions you encountered. (e.g., fear, joy, etc.)

_____

_____

_____

_____

_____

_____

_____

_____

♥   How did this make you feel?

_____

_____

_____

_____

_____

_____

_____

_____

_____

_____

_____

Reflections
FROM JOANNA

Great job!

As your mindset shifts, you'll be amazed at the opportunities that will present itself to you. I'm proud of you for reading this chapter and doing your homework! Keep on keeping on. As you begin to see things about yourself that make you go "OUCH!" it is important for you to acknowledge and accept them and to be encouraged that you can now make good changes. You are very courageous to do this!

Are you ready to explore the next milestone to unlock the keys of freedom and blessings in your life? In the next chapter, we are going to talk about the power of receiving a blessing and the power of your inner mirror. Many women don't understand how these two things plays a vital role in attracting and keeping a good man. Let alone opening the doors of breakthrough.

Are you ready? Let's do this!

Chapter Two
THE BEAUTIFUL YOU

When you're alone in front of the mirror, what are your secret feelings about yourself? Do you struggle with unworthiness? Are you struggling with self-body shaming? Do you have trouble feeling worthy? Are you having trouble with the aging process? Are you unable to receive a compliment? Do the words *"If only I were this . . . "* or *"If only I were that . . ."* wage a war in your mind?

If you answered "Yes" to any of these questions, you are not alone. I've been there and done that. Now is your time to shift this within yourself. If I did it, you can too!

Before we discuss the mistakes women make that repel good men, the inner self-mirror is the second foundation stone we need to address. Your identity and how you see yourself lie at the core of your world. They drive all that you do. Based on my personal experience and as a seasoned speaker, I would say this is the number one issue women struggle with.

A good exercise to employ daily is to stand six feet away from the mirror and repeat, "I am beautiful. I am loved." From this distance, you aren't focused on your imperfections, and it replaces negative thinking with positive affirmations.

There is scientific evidence that the brain changes when we tell ourselves affirming words.

**There is power in agreement. There is power in words.
There is power in receiving a blessing.**

Words create and build up. Words tear down and destroy. As women, we don't hear enough about how amazing, beautiful, and special we are. Often, we experience the opposite—negative words that tear us down.

During our youth, our self-views are formed by numerous factors. It might be negative words from one of your parents. It could be a parent who is emotionally or physically absent. Perhaps it came from the perfectionism of your mom or dad. It could stem from bullying by other kids.

These various scenarios create the "old tapes" or voices from the past that play repeatedly in our subconscious. Then, negative situations occur as adults that add to the old tapes and further damage our souls. Our identity as a woman is stolen by it. As a result, the inner mirror of confidence, self-worth, and self-respect becomes distorted. We believe certain lies about ourselves, such as *"I'm ugly"* or *"I'm not smart (pretty, good) enough."*

Our response can be jealousy, backstabbing, manipulation, lies, or control. The men in our relationships may bear the brunt of our wounds. And what's the root of all these things? Unhealed hurt and trauma (big or small).

This was me. Part of my healing began with learning to receive a blessing and learning to forgive myself. It was hard at first, but I made myself do it. And I want to help you do this right now.

The definition of a "blessing," according to the Webster-Merriam Dictionary, is the act or words of one that blesses. So, let's start with a blessing over you. Will you allow me to bless you now before we deep dive into this chapter?

Please put your hand over your heart and say out loud, *"I give myself permission to receive my blessing."* Some may want to add: *"and forgive myself!"* Say it one more time. *"I give myself permission to receive my blessing [and forgive myself]."* Ok, now I want you to **SHOUT IT** one more time, ***"I give myself permission to receive my blessing [and forgive myself]!"***

Great job! Now, open your hands and receive this blessing:

I speak healing to your soul, heart, mind, and emotions.
I speak healing to your body and spirit.
I break off all negative words and word curses
that were spoken over you
and command them to leave your soul now.
I release new eyes to see yourself in the mirror
as a beautiful daughter of heaven.
I bind blessings and goodness over your life
and ask love to fill and heal you.
I declare that you are beautiful inside and out.
I declare you are worthy.
You are accepted, loved, honored, and cherished.
You are strong and courageous.
There is everything right about you!

How did reading these words make you feel? Give yourself permission to heal and receive. Allowing yourself to receive this blessing will help you learn how to have a successful relationship with a good man. It will also unlock other untold wonderful things to happen in your life like it did for me.

My first step in the healing process was learning how to love myself, to forgive myself, and to have compassion for myself. It allowed me to:

- ♥ Give myself grace.
- ♥ Honor my courage.
- ♥ Embrace my weaknesses with empathy.
- ♥ Appreciate the qualities that make me unique.
- ♥ Believe that ALL things are possible.

The fact that you have read this far shows that you are courageous and ready for new results to happen to you. I'm so proud of you!

Did you know that the definition of a "princess" is one who stands strong and courageous? She takes dominion over her land. This is you!

Maybe you have never thought of yourself as a princess. But guess what? You are strong and courageous, and you are taking dominion over your land by being open and willing to change your life.

Based upon this definition of a princess, I invite you to meditate on receiving this concept about yourself. Think about all the times you have had to be strong or courageous in your life.

The next thing to learn is to accept and forgive yourself with compassion. Here's a visual of the core principle of identifying the negative thought or belief, discrediting it, and creating a new belief.

I'm going to teach you an exercise that helped shift my mindset on multiple levels. Remember, awareness is the key to change. This method helped positively shift my mindset about everything from relationships to finances. Throughout the day, I jotted down all the negative thoughts that went through my mind. When I reviewed the list, I stared in disbelief at the pages and pages of negativity.

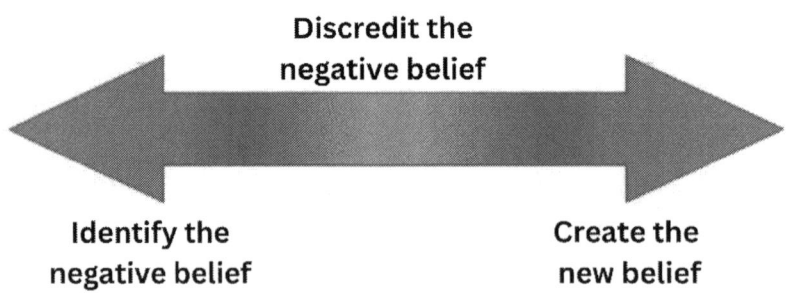

**Discredit the
negative belief**

**Identify the
negative belief**   **Create the
new belief**

CHANGING THE INNER MIRROR TECHNIQUE

♥ **Step #1:** Create awareness by identifying the negative thought. (inner voice).

♥ **Step #2:** Write down the negative thought. (I had three pages front and back!)

♥ **Step #3:** Write down a positive thought.

♥ **Step #4:** Verbally come out of agreement with the negative thought. e.g., *"I renounce and come out of agreement with the lie that says [negative thought]."*

♥ **Step #5:** Verbally agree and declare the positive thought. Speak it with energy from the belly. E.g., *"I attract* [   ]*"* or *"I am* [   ]*"* and so on. It must be a POSITIVE statement!

Completing this exercise left me shocked by my own negativity. And yes, I replaced each one of those negative thoughts from all three pages with a positive one, going through the entire exercise for each one. The fruit you will see in your life will make this worth it, I promise. If I did it, so can you!

A PERSONAL EXAMPLE

On a piece of paper, write two columns. One column will contain a negative statement (belief, feeling, etc.) about yourself. The second column will contain a positive statement. Denounce the negative statement audibly and proclaim the positive one audibly. When your ears hear each statement, your heart will begin to believe it and receive it.

A NEGATIVE THOUGHT, BELIEF, OR PATTERN	A POSITIVE THOUGHT, BELIEF, OR PATTERN
All the good guys are taken!	I attract great, emotionally healthy single men.

Speak out the declaration! I spoke this with passion from my belly, even when I didn't feel like it. Then, create a new belief declaration. For example:

- ♥ "I renounce and come out of agreement with the lie that all the good guys are taken!"
- ♥ "I ATTRACT GREAT, EMOTIONALLY HEALTHY, SINGLE MEN! The man of my dreams is waiting for me and can't wait to marry me!"

Woo hoo! You're doing this! Now, you have a practical tool for *any* negative thought about any subject or situation.

I completed this exercise about my finances and shocked myself yet again because it was three pages long! I still make it a habit to practice this exercise regularly to keep negative thoughts at bay.

Are *you* ready to do this exercise? There's no time like the present. So, complete your own chart below!

A NEGATIVE THOUGHT, BELIEF, OR PATTERN	A POSITIVE THOUGHT, BELIEF, OR PATTERN	A NEW BELIEF DECLARATION

If you think a spiritual healing prayer is necessary, please read Appendix A before proceeding.

Women are created to be nurturers. We are moms, grandmas, daughters, aunties, and friends who are leaders in our community and make silent sacrifices for our families. As a result, we may place ourselves last and often feel guilty for doing something for ourselves. It feels like there's an unwritten rule that you must prioritize everyone else before yourself. Unfortunately, this tends to be imbalanced most of the time.

I was what I just described at one time in my life. Everyone came to me for help. But when I needed help, there was rarely someone to support me after all I did for others. The experts call this "co-dependent," which can also be a form of self-hatred because we are ignoring our own needs. It can be a form of identity and purpose for our lives. Yep! I was all of the above for a time.

If you recognize varying forms of these behaviors in your life, congratulations— you are now on the road to victory! To break this cycle in my life, I also had to permit myself to love myself. Initially, this wasn't easy because I was so programmed the other way.

Right now, I'm asking you to do the same. It's very simple. Put your hand over your heart and say, "I give myself permission to forgive myself and others. I permit myself to love myself."

I'm so excited for you! You're rocking' this. Remember what I said in the beginning: There is power in words. There is power in agreement. There is power in receiving a blessing.

You now can receive the blessing opportunities waiting for you.

> *How you love yourself is how you teach others to love you.*
> RUPI KAUR, MILK AND HONEY

Reflections
FROM JOANNA

Excellent Work Just Now!

You've just completed two major milestones with Chapter One and Chapter Two!

I'm proud of you for reading this chapter and doing your homework! You've learned to do three life changing things. Love, forgive and give yourself permission to receive. You've just received the keys to freedom and blessings in your life.

You've also learned a life changing technique on how to identify the negative thought, discredit the old thought and create a new thought. You will declare your new thoughts with boldness and energy. Even when you don't feel like it.

Ready to discover another master key for great romance results? In the next chapter, we are going to talk about the power of a queen in the game of chess and in life she can be a kingmaker or man-breaker. Many women don't understand the importance of this role in attracting and keeping a good guy.

Are you ready? Let's go!

Chapter Three
THE MAN-BREAKER
Mistake #1

> *Women marry men, hoping they will change. Men marry women*
> *hoping they will not. Each is inevitably disappointed.*
>
> ALBERT EINSTEIN

Aren't we women waiting for that "perfect" man to come along? Aren't we often good at helping a guy change something about himself, especially *after* he's committed to the relationship? We're great at giving guys advice on how to improve things. We women know best, right?

All kidding aside, when it comes to romance results, nothing will repel a good man faster than:

- ♥ Making him feel like he's not good enough.
- ♥ Trying to change him.
- ♥ Finding something wrong with him, redoing his work, or negating his efforts to do something nice.
- ♥ Constantly one-upping him.
- ♥ Dismissing his compliments because you can't receive a compliment and think he's not sincere.

As a result, he feels rejected, like a failure, and defeated because no matter what he does, it's not good enough. From his perspective, why should he bother to keep trying because you're never happy?

Studying women who had a great relationship changed the way I did things. They had the results I wanted. I observed how she was treating her guy. What kinds of things would she say or not say? How she handled conflict with him.

Interestingly, what these women had in common was inner confidence, which was something I didn't have at that time in my life. They had a healthy mindset about men, enjoyed being around them, and weren't fearful of getting hurt. They set healthy boundaries rather than being controlling. Another thing these ladies had in common was being affirming and honoring their man, especially publicly. They are what I coined "**kingmakers**."

A kingmaker is a woman who has also learned how to affirm the superhero qualities in a man. The inner superhero in him represents his desire to be a protector, provider, and source of strength, and she celebrates those qualities. She is a woman who honors, respects, and accepts him for who he is. A kingmaker has learned how to appreciate, affirm, and validate his feelings.

Going back to the men I interviewed as part of my book research. I was pretty surprised to hear them echo the same message:

> **Good men want to be your hero. They want to please you.**

Interestingly, in the game of chess, the queen has the most influence on the board. She can take out any opponent and move in any direction to protect the king. She has a lot of power.

Every queen can use her influence for good or for bad. This means she can either be a kingmaker or a man-breaker. She can choose to use her power of influence for good to build up or bad to tear down. A good queen learns how to build up and protect her king.

In Chapter Two, we discussed how past traumas (big and small) can damage our inner mirror and can cause us to believe lies about ourselves and men. It can lead us to unconsciously punish men in general for what someone else did to you. These superhero deactivator behaviors repel the loving relationship we desire.

Left unchecked, these man-breaking behaviors and patterns of thinking damage good Mr. Potentials. How many times have you met a guy who would have been great, except that his ex had left him emotionally damaged?

There are a lot of good men out there. Regrettably, these good men bear the scars from instances where women deceived, stole, manipulated, controlled, and betrayed their trust. In life, there's the choice to be an outstanding role model or a horrible warning.

> **We can't change other people, but we can change our behaviors and responses. We can be a thermostat of influence for good. You don't want another woman to damage your Mr. Potential, and you don't want to be that woman. As we learn to become a queen, together, we will be kingmakers, not man-breakers.**

Your thoughts might still linger about how Mr. Wrong hurt you in the past and wondering why you should have to change. Let me ask you this: Are you happy with your current situation? Is what you've been doing so far working for you? Most likely, the answer is "no."

Be encouraged that focusing on your inner self in this journey of discovery and transformation will lead to beautiful changes, especially in the arena of meeting the love of your life. You deserve the best. You deserve to be a better version of yourself.

> *You must be the change you wish to see in the world.*
> GANDHI

THE MAN-BREAKER, AKA THE SHAMER

Let's look at the man-breaking behaviors of "**The Shamer**." The Shamer disrespects, belittles, or shames her man or men, whether in public or private. She makes him feel inadequate because she is fearful and insecure. Controlling behaviors are rooted in fear and insecurity.

She rarely thanks him for the things he has done or notices the little thoughtful things he did. She consistently talks over him, ensuring her irritation and anger about something he did or didn't do are clear to all within earshot.

A Shamer may dismiss her man's work, as well as the time and energy he has devoted to doing something for her (big or small), because she has an entitlement, *WIIFM* attitude. These behaviors often stem from control, unforgiveness, and bitterness.

These negative emotions are like weeds. What happens with weeds? They take root and have offshoots that spread under the soil. Eventually, they choke the life out of the healthy plants in the garden.

I've seen a lot of women who hold a grudge against *all* men from abuse as a child or betrayal from a man that they refuse to deal with. Or she may be angry with a man and hold a grudge for his past mistakes, disappointments, etc. As a result, the woman takes it out on the good Mr. Potential. He gets punished. i.e., You hurt me in the past, and I won't let it go (unforgiveness); therefore, you now owe me (entitlement), *and I'm going to make sure you pay for it* (revenge) every chance I get.

Because of her bitterness and unforgiveness, she makes him pay every chance she gets. Have you ever felt like that?

Let's look at a few extreme and subtle examples of the Shamer man-breaking behaviors. I believe it will be easy for you to spot and identify. You may even say, "Oops! I've done a minor or major form of this." Or you might think, [Insert a name] *does this and really needs to read this book!*

Have you ever witnessed a woman who makes fun of her man in front of others? Or she jokingly complains about how her husband is not this or not that? Have you ever been around a woman with a demeaning attitude toward her guy? Are these kingmaker behaviors or superhero deactivators?

A subtle put-down is still a put-down.

Shaming, whether blatant or subtle, is detrimental to a man's self-esteem and emotional well-being. Negative comments or actions that undermine his capabilities or masculinity can lead to feelings of inadequacy, emotional distancing, and resentment.

THE CONFERENCE SPEAKER SHAMER

I was at a major conference, seated in the back of the room. My chair was close to the book table of one of the female conference speakers who had just finished presenting. Her husband was doing an amazing job of handling her book table, taking orders, handling countless customer questions, helping with tech issues, and making sure she had everything.

She was a charming, attractive, and charismatic speaker. However, during her presentation, she subtly dishonored her husband by joking that he was the "wallpaper." The audience gave a nervous laugh because it wasn't funny. Oblivious to the audience's response, she continued to make veiled digs about his "shortcomings."

After her speaking session, she went to her book table to talk with people. Right in front of her customers, the speaker snapped at her husband about a minor snafu. She carried on treating him like a servant. Her snarky tone was painfully embarrassing to witness.

This speaker thought she was a queen and felt justified (entitlement) in treating her husband so poorly. However, everyone saw the pain and shame on his face, except her. I was shocked and could tell the others were thinking what I was thinking: *Wow, her behavior is really ugly!*

He was an attractive and pleasant gentleman. Those of us who witnessed her shaming behavior put our items down without purchasing. As good as her resource materials were, I wasn't going to support her man-breaking behavior.

As you just read, a man-breaker may think she's entitled to treat people in a demeaning way. However, those behaviors don't make a queen. They are damaging actions that can cause others to see her as the wicked witch instead. As the man-breaker, she leaves a trail of wreckage of hurting people behind her.

> *For every action, there is an equal and opposite reaction.*
>
> NEWTON'S THIRD LAW OF MOTION

What could this speaker have done differently? For starters, she could have publicly thanked her husband from the stage for all his hard work, time, and energy. She could have mentioned that without his tremendous support, she couldn't do what she does. Imagine how good he would have felt if she had done so. He would have been inspired to want to help her more because he was her superhero.

The speaker should never have corrected his minor mistakes in front of the customers, let alone with a snarky tone of voice. Who wants to be demeaned in front of others? It's especially humiliating for a man. What if he had done that to her? I guarantee you, he would have been in the doghouse! If she were a kingmaker, she would have graciously pulled him aside and brought it to his attention in a non-accusatory tone.

Remember the advice I shared previously: Little keys unlock big doors. Big doors swing on small hinges. What has resulted in doors you opened with shaming behaviors? How do you think others have felt by your stinging words? Do you:

- ♥ Have unresolved feelings from a past relationship?
- ♥ Have unhealed anger or resentment toward men?
- ♥ Always have to argue a point?
- ♥ Always have to be right?
- ♥ Always have to have the last word?
- ♥ Need to be in control in a relationship? And, deep down, are you afraid of getting hurt?

In the journey of my transformation, these are all questions I had to ask myself. The choice to make changes and become the kingmaker is what caused me to attract and keep a wonderful man like my husband, David. He is thoughtful and respectful, takes out the trash, compliments me, supports my gifts, is not selfish, and is very reciprocal.

Would I have attracted a good man like David if I were my old self? No! Instead, I allowed the spiritual mirror to reveal my inner reflection of selfish motivations. I humbled myself and learned from the various women who had what I wanted with a long-lasting, loving relationship.

> *If you want to be successful, find someone who has achieved*
> *the results you want and copy what they do,*
> *and you'll achieve the same results.*
> TONY ROBBINS

THE SELF-JUSTIFIED SHAMER

For 28 years, a woman we'll call "Tami" was married to her husband, Robert. Unfortunately, she had never dealt with her past sexual abuse. Nor with her rage, unforgiveness, and bitterness from a betrayal in her previous marriage. Yes, this bled into her current marriage.

Tami shamed and demeaned Robert for just about everything. She felt justified in her *WIIFM* behaviors because of her past hurts and his past mistakes. Making him feel diminished was a way to control him. He was shamed for not taking out the trash; the hedge wasn't cut right, and the car wasn't washed often enough, along with a list of everything else he didn't do right. He was told when to do *this* and when to do *that*.

In addition, she would diminish him in front of others by bringing up his shortcomings or what she perceived as his failures. People would stare at her in shock. Because of her self-centeredness, she thought they were staring at her because of *what her husband had do*ne rather than her own poor behavior. Tami was a grudge holder from things in her past, yet unwilling to examine herself. She wouldn't apologize for anything she had done to hurt him.

Even though he had asked for forgiveness for a past episode and had changed, she continuously brought it up. This is another form of control rooted in fear and insecurity. If your man made a mistake in the past and is truly sorry, there's no quicker way to drive him out of the house than by holding it over his head. If he makes a mistake, says he is sorry but continues to do it, that's a different story.

Tami felt justified in *her* right to do this. He could never win in this scenario, and nothing he did was good enough. By the way, he made his mistake eight years ago and never repeated it, but she would not let him forget it.

As a result, Robert would leave for hours or go on trips. Then Tami wondered why he was distant, angry, and always going everywhere else but home. Now he was a neglectful, moody husband on top of everything else. Poor her.

> *Better to dwell in the wilderness, than with a contentious*
> *(likely to cause disagreement or argument) and angry woman.*
> JOANNA'S INTERPRETATION OF PROVERBS 21:19, KJV

I had known Tami for over 13 years. One day, in her self-righteous frustration, she asked my advice about how to get Robert to change. I asked if she really wanted the truth, and she said, "Yes."

I said, "Are you sure?"

Tami definitively responded: "Yes. I'm sure! "

In a nutshell, I told her, "I've noticed that it seems like nothing he does is right, and he gets shamed for almost everything. Perhaps try affirming the things he does and tell him how you appreciate his efforts. Tell Robert what he did right, not what he did wrong."

I continued, "For example, when he does the dishes, don't criticize it, and redo it. Instead, thank him and make him feel good that he even thought about doing them. Men respond to sincere compliments. And here's one more thing to consider: Try honoring him in front of others instead of embarrassing him by pointing out his mistakes to them. This way, you build him up and not tear him down."

Do you think she liked my suggestions? Umm, not exactly!

She hated my suggestions and refused to change the way she was crushing his inner superhero. Then Tami stopped talking to me because she felt I had sided with him. She was unwilling to look at herself, deal with her pain, or change her ugly behavior. Their marriage continued to be miserable for them both, and last year, she unexpectedly passed away (natural causes) in bed at her home.

Guess what happened to her husband? He blossomed because he wasn't under the constant anger, control, bitterness, shaming, and belittling words.

A quick side note: It takes courage to look at yourself. You're doing great! It's your time to shine and get the romance results you desire. This will happen as you become aware, reflect, and meditate on where you need to make changes or adjustments. Keep on reading!

As I was interviewing various men for input on this subject, I had a shocking revelation! I found out that the only opinion a man cares about most is that of his woman. What? I'm going to repeat this point: **The only opinion a man cares about most is that of his woman.**

This means that when "his woman" jokes with subtle putdowns, chastises him publicly, or shames him, it's like stabbing him in the heart. Remember, a put-down is a put-down. Then we women wonder why he disappeared or told her, "I don't love you anymore," and ran off with a neighbor, co-worker, or friend.

THE SUBTLE CULTURAL SHAMING

How often have we heard or spoken the words, "Happy wife, happy life," or that a husband's last words should be "Yes, dear." Everyone laughs at those statements, but let's unpack this. What's the real underlying message of this quote?

The husband isn't important, and his voice doesn't matter. Remember the Barbie movie messaging? Barbie is living, and Ken is existing. Notice the subtlety in this. The quote is better rephrased as, "Happy spouse, happy house," inferring that *both* spouses are to make each other happy.

THE CASUAL SHAMER

A friend, whom we'll call "Mike," had a friend named "Don." Don was an obese man with a skin condition that caused major discoloration on his face. However, he was a kind, wonderful, and gentle soul who would give you the shirt off his back. In his lifetime, he had been severely bullied because of his weight and skin condition.

Mike's girlfriend saw a picture of his friend and made a careless and shaming comment about Don's appearance, stating, "Ewww! Who is that? He looks weird and ugly."

Mike stared at his girlfriend in shock. At that moment, he realized this relationship was over based on her cruel words. Mike understood that her heart's attitude was evident in her spoken words. He broke up with her, and she was clueless as to why.

How could Mike's girlfriend have handled it in a queenly way? If she had a concern about Don, she could have nicely said, "Oh, who is this friend? Tell me about him?" Then Mike would have shared about the trauma his friend had gone through. It would have given her the opportunity to show compassion. The outcome of their relationship could have been different.

> **Words create life and build up.**
> **Words tear down and bring death.**

What world are you creating with your words? The Bible says:

> *Death and life are in the power of the tongue."*
> PROVERBS 18:21A, KJV

As stated earlier, a fundamental truth is that a man places great importance on the opinion of his partner. The way a woman views and speaks about him profoundly impacts his self-perception. Positive affirmations, respect, and genuine appreciation from his woman provide him with the validation he seeks, strengthening the emotional bond between them.

In the realm of relationships, understanding and nurturing a man's efforts, sacrifices, and confidence are crucial for a healthy and fulfilling partnership. This journey involves avoiding man-breaking behaviors that shame or belittle him and recognizing and appreciating his efforts.

In addition, acknowledging and valuing his efforts, whether in big or small gestures, can create a positive atmosphere that encourages him to continue investing in the relationship. It empowers his inner superhero. By avoiding shaming behaviors, embracing his efforts, understanding the weight of a woman's opinion on his self-esteem, and empowering his inner superhero, a relationship can thrive.

Effective communication, genuine appreciation, and mutual respect form the foundation of partnership. These actions and behaviors foster an environment where love can blossom and grow. This is what I have found with my husband David and myself. We both try to be the best versions of ourselves.

Here are some action items to help you in the journey of awareness and changing patterns:

♥ **Make it a practice to use your words to create life and build up.** Don't use them to tear down, demean, or shame. Make it your intention to notice the actions (big or small) that are good, thoughtful, or nice. For example, if you are at a public location and a man opens the door for you, acknowledge him with a smile and thank him. Notice his response when you do this. As you do this more and more, you'll be amazed at how things shift.

♥ **Begin to make it a habit to look for the positive first and resist giving your opinion on the way you think it should be.** Refrain from pointing out what wasn't done correctly. Affirm what was done right. For example, affirm behaviors/actions that show effort.

♥ **Become aware of cultural man jabs.** For example, make it a point to notice cultural man jabs or joking putdowns. Find a way to change the negative statement into a positive statement. Begin to make it a habit to see something positive to compliment, no matter how small.

♥ **Be willing to say *I'm sorry*.** As you reflect on this chapter and may have engaged in some ugly behaviors, now is the time to acknowledge them. Give yourself grace and dig deeper to explore the root of your fears, hurts, or insecurities.

If appropriate, go back to the person and take responsibility for any man-breaking behaviors. Affirm their positive attitudes. If it's not appropriate, write a letter that you won't send. You'll be amazed at the freedom you'll feel. **If you need a deeper healing or prayer on this, go to Appendix A**.

Creating awareness is key, and that's why doing the homework assignments is very important. You are beginning to retrain the way you think, respond, and view things. Remember from Chapter Two, it's crucial to forgive yourself and avoid feeling shame, guilt, or condemnation for any negative actions. This is accepting the good, bad, and the ugly about yourself. It's about understanding your inner motivations and being willing to change them. There are things in the past that helped contribute to the current perceptions about life, men, and yourself, and you're doing a beautiful job of going deeper! Keep it up!

HOMEWORK ASSIGNMENT:

Begin with three consecutive days and finish the following tasks:

1. Catch yourself on this: Don't correct anyone's way of doing things, even if you think it could be done differently or better. Write how many times you caught yourself wanting to correct someone else.

   Day 1_____ Day 2_____ Day 3_____

2. Look for subtle superhero deactivators in movies, conversations, sitcoms, videos, memes, etc. Write how many times you noticed subtle or obvious superhero deactivators/man putdowns, as this creates awareness.

   Day 1_____ Day 2_____ Day 3_____

3. Be intentional and look for something you can make a positive comment on with people you don't know. Complimenting someone you don't know will

help you step out of your comfort zone. It also enables you to create awareness when someone does something good, nice, or positive.

For example, it could be at the grocery store cashier, salon, dentist, doctor's office, restaurant server, department store, etc. If the cashier was polite or a server did something nice, let them know you really appreciate their excellent service. Note their expressions, then journal your experiences, thoughts, and feelings. Record what came up for you as you did this exercise.

_____

_____

_____

_____

_____

_____

_____

_____

_____

To move forward with new results, we need to examine honestly the root cause of our motivations. It's a crucial step before you can progress with change and understanding.

> *Change is hard at first, messy in the middle,*
> *and gorgeous at the end.*
> ROBERT SHARMA

In the following table, there are two columns: A and B. List the behaviors (big and small) in Column A that you used to or currently engage in. In Column B, identify the root cause or subconscious lie you believe has influenced that action.

For example, you might write "Controlling" in Column A. Think about what caused you to be controlling. Was it fear or insecurity? What false beliefs do you hold about yourself? Were you abandoned, betrayed, or lied to by a past ex, etc., that caused the feelings? What promises did you break? The key is to gain an understanding of your inner motivations for making the choices and taking the actions you have and do.

This exercise is critical because it will give you a starting grid of understanding for those deeper wells within your heart. Please take the time to do this right now while you're here. I promise your work efforts will pay off like they did for me!

Directions: *Write out the list of man-breaking behaviors and your broken promises and identify the underlying root cause of these behaviors/choices.*

Column A Man-Breaking Behaviors	Column B Underlying Root Cause

List the common denominators/themes you have noticed.

_____

_____

_____

_____

_____

_____

_____

_____

_____

_____

_____

Now, go back to the end of Chapter Two and do the Inner Mirror Technique. Compile a list of the lies that came up in this exercise, and then continue with the Inner Mirror process.

I applaud you! Keep reading; you're doing a fantastic job!

> *Man cannot discover new oceans unless he has*
> *the courage to lose sight of the shore.*
> ANDRE GIDE

Reflections FROM JOANNA

Great job!

You are embarking on the journey of becoming a kingmaker. Congratulations!

I'm so proud of your inner work so far! You've learned how to appreciate thoughtful acts, affirm positive behaviors and a recognize efforts. You're becoming aware of the inner motivations of your heart and taking responsibility. You are learning how to use your words to build up and not tear down.

It's a new day!

Ok, are you ready to learn another way to affair proof your relationship (future or current)?

In the next chapter, we are going to discuss a superhero deactivator that would seem like the most unlikely superhero behavior that repels a good man.

Are you ready? Let's go!

Chapter Four
THE REVERSE TRAINER
Mistake #2

> *I can live for two months on a good compliment.*
>
> MARK TWAIN

Everyone appreciates a sincere compliment, but how many of us can graciously receive one without negating it or feeling like we have to compliment someone back?

Although my journey of singleness was quite long and full of mistakes, it was the best education I could have ever received. As we explore the significant mistakes that repel good men and how to reverse them, what I'm about to share next may be a big surprise. It's what you would call a "little key that unlocks a big door."

A light bulb went on in my head, realizing that rejecting a compliment is the equivalent of being a "**Reverse Trainer.**" You're thinking, *what is a Reverse Trainer?* I'm glad you asked.

> **When the inability to receive outweighs the ability to give, we are Reverse Trainers.**

A reverse trainer is someone who trains others how to stop giving compliments or gifts. She calls negative attention to herself and inadvertently blocks her blessings. You might wonder how that is possible. Let's find out!

At one point, we have all operated at higher or lower degrees as the reverse trainer. Every woman may carry a secret insecurity about herself in one form or another. It could be her weight, height, body shape, hair, face, breast size, or skin. Others of us may struggle with not feeling smart enough, pretty enough, worthy enough, creative enough, or good enough, or having an inability to recognize our uniqueness.

These insecurities, combined with feelings of unworthiness and subconscious self-hatred, can greatly contribute to the inability to receive.

Let's do a quick evaluation:

- ♥ Do you have a hard time accepting a compliment?
- ♥ If someone compliments you, do you immediately feel the need to compliment that person back?
- ♥ Does it feel awkward when someone gives you a gift, and you feel obligated to give them a gift in return?
- ♥ Is your identity rooted in being the rescuer, the victim, or the problem-solver?
- ♥ When someone says you look pretty, do you negate the compliment because you believe that you're ugly?

One of the most significant areas I've seen women struggle with (including myself in the past) is learning to receive an honest compliment or gift. They find it difficult to accept the compliment as true, or appreciate and value it.

I want to share a quick story David (my husband) told me about. He was visiting someone in the hospital. Walking down the hallway, he saw a woman pushing a medical cart. He suddenly felt the holy presence of God, and a thought went through his mind. God whispered, "They are all pretty to me."

The reverse trainer struggles with an inability to receive a compliment (gift of esteem, respect, affection, or admiration). The difficulty of receiving can lead to blocking other blessings in her life and pushing good people away.

> **I'll say it once again! Little keys unlock big doors
> and big doors swing on small hinges.**

A quick side note: We are **not** talking about flattery, which is excessive and insincere praise used for manipulation.

Let's look at Webster's definition of a compliment: "The expression of esteem, respect, affection, or admiration." **In essence, a compliment is a gift of esteem, respect, affection, or admiration.** If someone gives you a sincere compliment, is it good or bad? It's good. So why do we reject it?

How does rejecting compliments contribute to your man potentially straying from your relationship or repelling a good guy? Read on.

I once attended a conference where the guest speaker made a statement that has stuck with me to this day. She said, **"We train people how to treat us, either good or bad (allowing disrespect)."**

The most common roots of the inability to receive are a subconscious form of unworthiness, fear of being hurt, perfectionism, and low self-esteem. It can also be rooted in a form of distrust of men from past hurts or abuse that hasn't been healed or dealt with yet. I had to heal from that before I could learn how to receive and address my inability to receive. My next book will focus on healing your inner identity from abuse, which is a more in-depth subject.

As the Reverse Trainer, we train (teach) people how to dishonor us. We reject compliments, gifts, or acts of kindness. We also may tolerate unjust and negative attitudes toward us. The fruits of the inability to receive often result in self-sabotaging our relationships and blessings.

These superhero deactivators repel good men and sabotage healthy relationships. Inadvertently, this imbalance in our ability to receive leads us to become **blessing blockers**.

You may be wondering how not receiving a compliment is a blessing blocker. Allow me to elaborate. Think of a compliment as a gift. When someone gives you a compliment, they are happy to provide you with this gift. Most people like to give compliments because it makes them feel good.

By rejecting the compliment (gift), the Reverse Trainer rejects the person who gave the gift. She unknowingly repels love, relationships, opportunities, and people. Essentially, she's telling the Universe she doesn't want a gift. This can include blocking answers to prayers because she's rejecting the gift.

Basically, she's holding her hand up to the heavens, saying, "I don't deserve it, I don't want it. Give the blessings to someone else because I chose not to accept it." As a result, she's most likely the one who gives and gives, never receives, and becomes resentful. Sound familiar?

In the past, when a guy complimented me, I'd reject the compliment (essentially calling him a liar). For example, one time, I was at a social gathering, and a nice man engaged me in conversation. We had a great exchange of equal give and take until he complimented me on my outfit. Because I was struggling with feeling bloated that day, I said, "Oh, you're just saying that; look how bloated my stomach is, and this is an old outfit."

Shocked at my response, he stared at me and didn't know what to say. Because he was sincere, he perceived my response as rude and a personal rejection. He politely excused himself, and I couldn't understand why he didn't ask for my number.

How many times have you done this? Let's identify the superhero deactivators in my example. I inadvertently did several things in a single moment: 1) I called him a liar. 2) I rejected his gift (compliment). 3) I drew negative attention to my body (he didn't notice my bloated stomach. And 4) I called myself a poor dresser.

I effectively trained him to mistreat me and look for the undesirable things about my body. Yes, I was The Reverse Trainer.

What were my romance results? I repelled him. Imagine how he would have felt if I had responded with the opposite response of, "Thank you so much! I receive that," and flashed a big smile at him. Most likely, he would have asked me out. He would have felt appreciated, honored, and happy that I received **his** gift. Isn't this response more appealing to a man than "I look fat, and you're just saying that?"

Let's do a little deeper dive into this: In part, my identity was rooted in being the one who helped everyone, instead of seeing myself as royalty. I was a rescuer, a problem solver, a go-to for prayer requests, and a leader, but I couldn't receive for myself. It was a form of self-protection rooted in fear. In addition to being co-dependent, it gave me a false sense of being in control. Basically, it was a form of pride in playing the martyr. It also was a cover-up not to have to deal with myself. If I'm out helping everyone else, I don't have to look inside of myself.

Women are natural nurturers and givers. It's one trait that makes us unique and different from men. We are born with the ability to have babies, love others, and raise our children. **However, when the inability to receive outweighs the ability to give, we become reverse trainers.**

One day, while in prayer, God showed me an illustration that revealed the negative way I was affecting people with my inability to receive. In my mind's eye, I saw a scene of me taking the time to pick out a beautiful floral bouquet for my best friend. I looked for the right colors and fragrances of the flowers and put a lot of thought into this gift to cheer her up.

In the next scene, I handed her the beautiful flower bouquet. She took it from me, looked at it, scowled, and then slapped me in the face with it. The petals flew everywhere. I could see the look of shock and sadness on my face because she rejected my gift—ultimately rejecting me. Then I felt angry because of her rudeness. Did I want to give her any other gifts? No.

The Holy Spirit spoke to my heart, "This is how you make people feel when you don't accept the gift of their compliment. They feel rejected, disrespected, sad, and angry. They won't want to bless you anymore. If you can't even receive a compliment, how can you receive the blessings of heaven?"

How does a genuine queen receive a gift? **She accepts it with grace and gratitude, making the giver feel good about giving the gift.**

Wow, talk about a piercing zinger of truth! I was repelling good people and healthy love. I was rejecting them, making them feel bad, and ultimately robbing them of their blessing from giving. At that moment, I decided to change. I made it an intention to learn how to receive a compliment without giving one back and simply say, "Thank you, I receive it."

As I began to practice the new superhero activator behaviors, I noticed how happy the expressions on people's faces were when I thanked them and appreciated their gift (compliment). **They were happy because I was accepting their gift, and it made THEM feel good to give.**

Most of the time, we don't realize that we're training others (especially men) to stop complimenting us, stop desiring us, stop buying flowers, or stop doing nice things. We don't realize that we're rejecting their gifts, calling them liars, and fault-finding.

Let's look at some additional Reverse Trainer examples and the messaging behind the actions.

FIRST SCENARIO:

Friend: "I love that sweater on you; it fits you well." (a compliment is a gift)

Reverse Trainer: "Oh no, this thing is old." (refuting their opinion).

    "I bought it on sale a few years ago." (drawing negative attention to yourself).

    "I love the top that YOU are wearing." (rejecting the gift and returning it to sender).

Messaging to the Compliment Giver: *You're lying about the sweater and my body. I have poor taste in clothes, and you can't treat me nice, but I can treat you nice.*

SECOND SCENARIO:

Boyfriend: "You look great." (compliment)

Reverse Trainer: *"You're just saying that."* (calling him a liar).

    "I look fat." (cursing yourself).

Messaging to the Compliment Giver: *You're a liar; I hate myself, and you probably should, too!*

THIRD SCENARIO:

Husband: "I surprised you with flowers!" (a gift).

Reverse Trainer: "Why did you waste money to buy me these flowers? (*"I'm not worth it"*).

    "What do *you* want?" (Rejection of his gift and accusing him of an ulterior motive).

Messaging to the Compliment Giver: *Shame on you for wasting money on me. Spend it on someone else next time. I don't trust you to tell the truth and won't believe you when you do.*

FOURTH SCENARIO:

Husband: "How do you like the Victoria's Secret gift?"
Reverse Trainer: "What is this?" *(You shouldn't be thinking about me).*
      "You only bought this lingerie because you have an ulterior motive."
      (You're untrustworthy. I don't appreciate you. What you bought is bad).
      "All you want is sex." *(I'm not attracted to you sexually).*
Messaging to the Compliment Giver: *I don't appreciate that you desire me and thought enough about me to go to the store and buy me beautiful lingerie. I reject you sexually, your gift, and I don't want to have sex with you. Buy lingerie for another woman and think about having sex with her instead.*

LET'S TRANSLATE THIS INTO MAN LANGUAGE:

When he compliments you, and you don't believe it, why would he keep complimenting you? You have now engaged a superhero deactivator and are training him not to appreciate you. Does this behavior endear him to you or repel him?

My husband said that during his single years, it was **rare** for a woman he dated to receive his sincere compliments. He also said it became very irritating, frustrating, and tiresome when his compliments were consistently rejected and disbelieved. Is this you?

Imagine how good your man (future man) will feel when you smile with appreciation and say, "Thank you, I receive it" or "I appreciate it." Imagine how he'll be inspired to buy you more flowers when you thank him and receive the pretty bouquet he took the time to buy for you. Imagine when he does something nice for you, and you smile and honor him by accepting his gift.

These responses show honor and appreciation and make the other person feel special because you received their gift. Learning this skill will attract love, healthy people, and opportunities instead of repelling them. It can help draw Mr. Potential to you and set you apart from other women who don't know how to accept a gift.

This journey of transformation is about getting honest with yourself, creating an awareness of the things that need to change, and learning how to do them differently. You are discovering how to embody the good qualities of a queen. A queen knows how to receive as well as give. Great job! Keep reading.

The key to better romance results is awareness of where you are currently, identifying what needs a shift, and then practicing the new behavior patterns. I highly recommend you practice these with friends, family, etc. If you are in a relationship, practice them with your husband, boyfriend, or fiancée.

GRACIOUS, QUEENLY WAYS TO RECEIVE THAT BLESS OTHERS

- ♥ Allow others (him) to open the door for you, pull out your chair, carry something, help you in some way, or do an act of kindness for you. Become aware every time someone does this. Smile and say, "Thank you."
- ♥ Believe someone when they complement you. Refrain from rejecting the speaker and the compliment with a negative comment about yourself.
- ♥ Make them feel blessed with your gratitude and accept the compliment with a simple "Thank you. I receive that. How thoughtful; how kind of you," etc.
- ♥ Notice their response when you thank them with a smile.

HOMEWORK ASSIGNMENT:

Are you ready? Your assignment is to learn how to be a good receiver.
Let's start by permitting yourself to receive.
Place your hand on your heart (skin to skin) and say, "I give myself permission to receive all the good gifts and blessings Heaven has for me." Say this **three** times with your hand on your heart.

Great job! Now, you are ready for the challenge.

CHALLENGE:

For the next five days, you're **only** to receive a compliment, gift, or a kind gesture someone may do for you. For example, let's say you are at the store, and someone opens the door for you. Smile and honor that person with an expression of appreciation. Then, observe how the other person responds to you.

You are **not** to compliment the person back, return the favor, or give them a gift in return. **This is an exercise in learning to receive.**

♥ **Journal your experience.** How did you feel about allowing someone to bless you? Was it hard or easy? How many times did you stop yourself from returning the compliment?

_____

_____

_____

_____

_____

_____

_____

_____

At one point, we've all operated in higher or lower degrees of the Reverse Trainer. The key to better romance results is creating awareness of where you are currently at, identifying what needs to be adjusted, and then practicing new patterns of behavior.

You are on the right path. I know you'll notice beautiful changes in your life as you implement the skills you're learning.

I'm so proud of you!

Reflections FROM JOANNA

You're doing awesome!

Congratulations, you finished another chapter!

In this session, you learned the key of accepting a compliment and how it unlocks big doors of blessings or rejection. You're becoming aware of man language and how to make him feel good about giving you his gift (compliment).

You're gaining wisdom on how to teach people to treat you with honor, in essence honoring yourself.

The best is yet to come!

Have you ever wondered why Mr. Potential becomes distant and withdrawn? Why he suddenly disappears? Or what could make him suddenly loose respect for you?

In the next chapter, you're going to find out one of the BIG mistakes women make that repel good men in this area, how to handle the distancing and how to reverse the man mistakes when it happens. Keep reading, and I'll meet you there.

Are you ready? Let's go!

Chapter Five
THE DISGUISED DOORMAT
(AKA The Yes Syndrome)

Mistake #3

> *The most painful thing is losing yourself in the process of loving someone too much and forgetting that you are special, too.*
>
> ERNEST HEMINGWAY

Have you ever lost yourself in a relationship? Do you give up your personal power when you're with a man?

As a healthy relationship develops into something more serious, it's natural to have your lives intersect. And when you marry, the focus becomes living your lives *together*. However, we will discuss a detrimental form of enmeshment that contributes to one becoming **The Disguised Doormat.**

For example, let's say you seem to have a beautiful connection with a guy you're dating, and things are going great. As time goes by, you do more things together and find your lives converging into one road. Then, before you know it, you're doing things he likes to do. You develop friendships with his friends, and you become deeply connected to his world.

However, as things progress, you drop your hobbies, activities, friends, and the things that attracted him to you in the first place. Your purpose becomes primarily focused on meeting all of his needs, wants, and desires. You begin to lose your identity as you say "Yes" to everything. You become afraid to state your opinions that differ from his and ultimately make your entire world revolve around him. This, in turn, causes the loss of healthy boundaries between you.

If any form of this has happened to you, you are not alone. This happened to me. It's a very sneaky dynamic that can slowly creep up on you called the "*Yes Syndrome.*" You become what I refer to as "**The Disguised Doormat**."

Prior to marrying Mr. Wrong, I was dating Mr. Potential. When I first met Mr. Potential, I was witty, confident, and independent. He was a pilot, romantic, handsome, spontaneous, and fun. We had a fantastic connection, would banter back and forth, and I let him *chase me.* Eventually, we started dating, and he would plan some of the most incredible surprise dates for me.

For example, one time, he had a red carpet with flower petals on it that led to the private Cessna plane. Then he flew me to another city for dinner at a restaurant on the water. Another time, he took me flying during the 4th of July so that I could see all the fireworks over the entire horizon at the same time. He would serenade me with piano music and sing me a romantic version of *Happy Birthday.*

Needless to say, I fell in love with him. It sounds so perfect, right? As we became more serious, I unknowingly fell into the *Yes Syndrome* and became the Disguised Doormat. I slowly stopped going out with my friends and started hanging out at his house all the time. I was saying "Yes" to everything he wanted, slowly giving up my independence and becoming too dependent on him.

An interesting dynamic happened as I engaged in the "*Yes Syndrome*" and became the disguised doormat. The more available I became, the less available he became.

The more distant he became, the more I pushed to be with him out of fear of losing him. I didn't realize that I had lost myself in the relationship. I would consistently ask him if he was mad at me.

Ladies! This was a huge mistake! It was the icing on top of the cake he didn't want to eat. It drove him even further away from me.

What makes a diamond so valuable? It's not easily obtainable.

Side Note: When your man is quiet, there can be many reasons that have nothing to do with you. He could just be processing some things from work, financial situations, stressful situations, etc. So, if he goes quiet, let him. Avoid and resist the fear factor of thinking you did something wrong. If you *know* you did something wrong, that's a different story.

Back to the pilot: He was not attracted to my new behaviors of fear or the *Yes Syndrome* rooted in my neediness and insecurity. What was the outcome? As you might guess—he left me for another woman who was not the disguised doormat. She had no problem calling him out, setting her foot down when needed. She was not afraid of abandonment or rejection. Being confident and secure, she did not constantly ask if he was mad or what he was thinking about.

Let's look at specific behaviors that attract a good guy. **Men are attracted to women who smile, have joy, emit confidence, and come across as open and friendly.** Men are also attracted to women who set and maintain healthy boundaries for themselves. They love a woman who knows how to stand her ground respectfully. She's not afraid to say "I'm not available" when needed.

They appreciate a woman who respects their mental man cave and doesn't constantly ask, "Are you mad at me?" or "What are you thinking?" Healthy men want a woman who clearly communicates her needs. They respond to a woman who knows how to validate his strengths and appreciate his efforts.

Healthy men are not attracted to women who pursue them. Most of the time, they become unattracted when the woman becomes the doormat. The more she operates in the *Yes Syndrome*, the more he begins to lose respect for her. They're also not attracted to women who come across as jealous, insecure, fearful, desperate and constantly need his validation.

WHO IS THE DISGUISED DOORMAT?

She is strong and independent and can hold her own until she gets involved with a man. When she gets into a relationship, she seems to lose her identity and moves into "fear of losing him" mode. His hobbies become her hobbies; she becomes the *"Yes. I'm available anytime that's convenient for you"* type. She takes on the role of a doormat.

When it comes to him, she puts her personal needs aside. She's still successful with everything else. Inadvertently, she becomes the man-pleaser in the relationship. She may begin to coddle and take care of things for him like a mother. She may do whatever he says to please him at the expense of her own needs. She becomes insecure about where he's going and who he's meeting.

Typically, this is rooted in a form of fear, unworthiness, low self-esteem, and a well-masked lack of identity within herself. He is initially attracted to her confidence and independence. However, as she begins to allow her world to be absorbed and focused on his world in an unhealthy way, he loses respect for her. The result? He distances himself.

As he pulls away, her fear and insecurity can go into overdrive. She tries to please him even more, not realizing her behaviors start to repel him. She may then resort to controlling him in passive/aggressive ways by doing something she knows will subtly hurt or irritate him. In order to win his love, she may resort to tactics such as sex, manipulation, or seeking revenge.

Emotionally healthy men will typically distance themselves and exit this kind of relationship. He is driven away by neediness and insecurity. That's what happened to me with the pilot.

If he's not emotionally healthy, there are a couple of directions this can go. He may start to operate in subtle or obvious forms of negative behavior against you. He may criticize, cheat on you, or become abusive.

A former colleague encountered this situation. We'll call her "Cheryl." Prior to meeting and marrying her ex-husband, she was independent and a successful therapist, and she enjoyed an excellent social life with wonderful friends. She met and started dating Mr. Potential, who seemed sophisticated, funny, well-traveled, and a savvy businessman. They hit it off and eventually got married.

As time progressed, she began operating in the *Yes Syndrome* and started only to do things he wanted to do. She stopped going out with her girlfriends and became dependent upon him. Cheryl went from being the confident, independent, free-spirited woman that initially attracted him to the Disguised Doormat.

In response, Mr. Potential lost respect for her. He started putting her down to test her reactions subtly. When she ignored his digs, he began to nitpick and complain about things even more. In response, she would try harder to be better.

She would say "Yes" to what he said and everything he wanted to do to please him. Eventually, things escalated to where he began cheating on her, yet she still looked the other way. Everything finally came to a crescendo when she had had enough and told him to pack his bags and get out. This was her second marriage, with an identical pattern.

How is it that when she's single, she maintains healthy boundaries with men? She is independent, has good friends, and has her hobbies. The minute she's in a relationship, she operates in the *Yes Syndrome* as the Disguised Doormat. Why?

Deep down, the Disguised Doormat most likely doesn't realize her true worth and value. She may be afraid of being alone due to past rejection. She may believe subconscious lies that cause her to sacrifice her self-respect. There's a chance that she is out of touch with herself. Maybe it's fear of getting hurt that drives her to controlling behaviors. Or, it could be the opposite, and she has a victim mentality. She can attract a guy but can't keep a good one.

One quick observation about the disguised doormat: Sometimes, being the disguised doormat is a way to get attention. For example, if the guy starts disrespecting her, and she allows it by not speaking up, then she's enabling him to treat her poorly. Then she calls her friends, telling them how poorly her man's treating her, and they give her sympathy. They respond with, "Oh, you poor thing. He's being terrible to you, and you are so nice to him."

Remember, we train people how to treat us.

If she calls him out and he continues to disrespect her and won't take responsibility for his actions, then she must make a choice about the relationship.

MY NEMESIS

I used to have a boss who would demean me, speak to me in condescending tones, and call out my mistakes in a public meeting. I would drive home in tears every day. Despite fervently wishing and praying, I couldn't find a different job. People would say, "Oh Joanna, I'm so sorry he's so awful to you. It must be so hard. You are such a hard worker and don't deserve to be treated this way. He is such a jerk!"

What kind of subconscious emotional payoff was this in my mind's eye? It was attention, validation, and recognition. It was also passive/aggressive behavior because now he looked bad, and I was the innocent victim.

Things finally came to a head when a co-worker pulled me aside. She looked me square in the eye and said, "Can I be honest with you about something?"

My heart started beating faster as I apprehensively looked at her and nodded with a "Yes."

She asked if I had heard what other people were saying about me. I shook my head softly with a "No."

Then she said, "Joanna, people talk about what a doormat you are and how you are afraid to stand up for yourself."

A part of me was shocked and stared at her in disbelief, but deep down, I knew they were right. She continued, "What beliefs do you have that cause you to be silent when your boss treats you the way he does? What are you afraid of? Do you enjoy the negative attention you get by complaining because you're not willing to do anything about it?"

Can you say "OUCH!?" As hard as it was to hear those words, I am eternally grateful because it caused me to make changes and learn new skills. Over time, I identified all the areas where I was being a doormat. I evaluated why I was allowing my boss (and others) to disrespect me. Was it fun to see the ugly about myself? Uh no. However, it was liberating. I learned to look at the ugly parts of myself with love, compassion, and forgiveness.

Did I learn how to stand up to my former boss? Yes, I did! It took time, and I had to learn new crucial conversation skills. I never allowed him to disrespect me again.

So, let's bring this back to a romantic relationship. Healthy men (and people in general) are attracted to inner confidence, which emits a positive frequency rather than the fearful frequency that can emerge when in the relationship. On the frequency scale, fear has the lowest frequency. A woman who truly knows her worth will stand out like a diamond to a good man.

I love meeting different people on my travels. One woman, whom we'll call "Jane," went through a phase in her marriage where she became the Disguised Doormat. It's easy to do when you have kids, animals, and a husband to take care of. Relationships go through different seasons. During one of these seasons, Jane's husband became distant, standoffish, and moody. She tried to connect with him in various ways, making suggestions on things they could do.

She tried to please him and make him happy, but the harder she tried, the snarkier he got. The more she reached out to him, the more he was hanging out with his friends. Finally, she pointedly asked what his problem was. He complained that she was always trying to change him and was constantly needing his attention.

She contacted me and asked what she should do. I suggested she stop making him the focus and spend time with friends and do fun things for herself. At last, on New Year's Eve, she had reached her limit and took my advice, leaving him behind and celebrating on her own. Without informing him of her whereabouts, she spent the weekend at a girlfriend's house which caused him to sweat a little by her not answering the phone. She took a stand and pulled away, allowing them both space to think and ultimately leading to a positive conversation.

What happened when she stopped trying to be the man-pleaser, and **he** was no longer **her** focus? As an emotionally healthy man, he realized what a jerk he was being and apologized to her. He's been respectful ever since. She's made it a point to continue her independent activities, go work out, have girlfriend time, etc.

Because she was stuck in the *Yes Syndrome*-man pleasing behaviors, her husband took her for granted. She annoyed him because she was too absorbed in his world. Once she pulled back, he had space to think. As a healthy guy, he took responsibility, apologized, and stopped doing disrespectful behaviors.

If you realize that you're engaging in a victim mentality and doormat behaviors, then it's time to STOP, pull back, and evaluate yourself. Begin to disentangle yourself from his world and begin to focus on yours. It might feel like the opposite thing to do, but it's important, as you saw in Jane's example.

THE MILLION-DOLLAR QUESTION

Why do you allow him to become your focus? Why don't you stand up for yourself? What do you really believe about yourself that causes you to be a man-pleaser as the disguised doormat? What are you afraid of?

As you take focus off him, it gives him room to breathe and not be under pressure from you. A healthy man doesn't want you to lose yourself in the relationship. Sometimes, guys need space, and taking pressure off a guy will go a long way. As women, we have to back off and be secure in ourselves.

THE WEDDING IS OFF

After David and I got engaged, we set a wedding date, and I started all the wedding preparations. At that time, we were dealing with his elderly parents' health issues. David called me one day and said he needed to stop the wedding plans because he was feeling stressed from caring for his ailing parents.

I had two choices on how to handle this. One option was to gloss over the stress he was feeling, go into "fear of losing him" mode, and pressure him for a different date. The other choice was to validate his feelings and support his parents' situation.

I chose the latter because I was secure in myself and not fearful. Marrying him wasn't going to change my identity because I knew my value and worth. I let him know that we'll cancel the wedding plans and go from there. He immediately felt the pressure come off and then came back the following week, saying he was okay with getting married on our original date. He appreciated the support I had given him. It endeared his heart to me even more.

As you begin your inner reflections, gain understanding, and focus on changing your responses and actions, you'll feel freedom as you come into new truths. Awareness will help you change your responses and take new, healthy actions.

> **Remember, you can't change anyone,**
> **but you can change the way you respond.**

As you practice your skills, it's amazing how others will respond differently to you. Everything is a choice. The key is to be willing to see.

> *You'll miss the best things if you keep your eyes shut.*
> DR. SEUSS

IMMEDIATE ACTIONS TO ADJUST DISGUISED DOORMAT BEHAVIORS

- ♥ Maintain your healthy friendships even after you are in a relationship. Find fresh connections or rekindle old ones.
- ♥ Make it an intention to celebrate you. Treat yourself to something nice/fun at least once a month. Once a week, if possible.
- ♥ Back off from the time that you spend initiating texts and talking with your man. Allow him to think about you and reach out to you.
- ♥ STOP being too available.
- ♥ If you have become immersed in his world, make it a point to step back and disconnect from his world. Take time to do your own thing, whether it's hanging out with your friends or family, traveling, hobbies, etc.

It's good that you have something you can do together. However, when you have been stuck in the unhealthy *Yes Syndrome*, it's important to take a break from spending so much time with him. Allow things to balance out and then maintain that balance.

- ♥ If you don't know who you are anymore, it's time to find out! Start with something simple, like taking a class of some kind that interests you. Learn a new language. Try a new activity and check out new groups of people. Step out of the comfort zone. Get to know yourself all over.
- ♥ Recognize where you have been operating in fear and putting pressure on your relationship. Fear causes us to control things.
- ♥ Acknowledge any victim mentality tendencies and start making changes now. Recognize any fear of abandonment, rejection, or man-pleasing tendencies.

INNER REFLECTIONS HOMEWORK ASSIGNMENT:

Now it's time to reflect honestly and write out the answers to the questions I'm about to ask you. It doesn't have to take a lot of time. Just quickly jot down the responses and then reflect upon your answers. I believe it will give you invaluable insights that will inspire growth and positive change in your life.

♥   Do you recognize any Disguised Doormat behaviors within yourself? If so, list them below.

_____

_____

_____

_____

_____

_____

_____

_____

_____

♥   Mark the statements that resonate with you.
   — Bad things always happen to me.
   — So and so made me feel this way.
   — There's nothing I can do about it. I can't because of_____.
   — It's not my fault these things keep happening to me.
   — Nobody cares about me.
   — I'm treated unfairly all the time.
   — There aren't any solutions to help me.
   — I'm not comfortable confronting someone who's disrespecting me.

These statements are possible indicators of a victim mentality. It's a mindset we rarely realize that we have. Things happen to you, and you can't control the outcomes. Others make you feel a certain negative way, and you need sympathy. If you recognize yourself in this area, great job! Awareness is the key to change.

> *No one can make you feel inferior without your consent.*
> ELEANOR ROOSEVELT

♥ Do you recognize any *Yes Syndrome* propensities within yourself? If so, what are some examples of your *Yes Syndrome* behaviors from a previous or in a current relationship?

_____

_____

_____

_____

_____

_____

_____

_____

♥ What fears or beliefs cause you to become the man-pleaser in the relationship?

_____

_____

_____

_____

_____

_____

_____

_____

♥ What kinds of things have happened in the past to make you feel like the disguised doormat? Do you still need healing?

_____

_____

_____

_____

_____

_____

_____

_____

♥ Are there subconscious lies that you aren't worthy, good enough, etc.? Describe them.

_____

_____

_____

_____

_____

_____

_____

♥ How do you truly see yourself? i.e., Is it as royalty? Or less than? Or perhaps not as good as? Is it as the person who doesn't deserve (unworthy) to have your needs met healthily?

_____

_____

_____

_____

_____

_____

_____

_____

_____

♥ What inner beliefs cause you to become entangled in his world and lose yourself?

_____

_____

_____

_____

_____

_____

_____

_____

_____

Great job on reading this chapter! I'm so proud of you! Keep going!

AFFIRMATIONS

Speak these aloud, with energy:

- ♥ I give myself permission to love and honor myself.
- ♥ I permit myself to say "No," which is an act of self-love.
- ♥ I come out of agreement with the fear of saying no.
- ♥ I release the need for approval from others and declare that I approve of myself, and it's enough.
- ♥ I renounce rejecting myself and choose to accept myself.
- ♥ I recognize that I cannot please everyone, and that's okay.
- ♥ I am strong, assertive, and true to myself; I am not a people-pleaser but a self-respecting individual.
- ♥ I attract people who respect my boundaries and value me for who I am.
- ♥ I give myself permission to attract healthy love and respect.
- ♥ I have the power to change any situation in my life!

Repeat these affirmations every day (as many times a day as needed) to help retrain your thinking. You can add your own. Doing this strengthens your commitment to maintaining healthy boundaries and not being a people-pleaser. Over time, they help you develop a stronger sense of self and healthier, more authentic relationships.

If you have trouble saying "No" to people, here's one of the responses I would say: "I would love to help, but I'm not in a position to do that right now."

> *The most common way people give up their power is by thinking they don't have any.*
> ALICE WALKER

♥ List three things that you are going to do to treat yourself kindly and with respect.

_____

_____

_____

_____

_____

_____

_____

_____

_____

_____

Chapter Six
THE QUEEN OF CHAOS

Mistake #4

> *Change starts with you. But it doesn't start until you do.*
>
> TOM ZIGLAR

Have you ever felt like your life was swirling like a tornado, whether it is finances, relationships, health, work, stress, emotional drama with an ex or family members, or fill in the blank? Does it seem like it's just one thing after another? Do you feel stuck, spinning and spinning, but getting nowhere?

I once saw a funny T-shirt that read, "Fueled by caffeine and chaos." How true is this at times?

However, let's look at when chaos becomes constant and can get us into trouble... We all go through seasons of feeling stuck in a tornado of chaos and having to process through those situations. Tornados represent instability that can turn in any direction at any time. Don't worry, you're not alone. Most of us have felt fueled by caffeine and chaos. Get ready for some exciting news—there's a breakthrough waiting for you!

It's when we unknowingly start spinning in a continuous cycle of chaos that it becomes an issue. We can become addicted to the drama of the tornado and become the "**Queen of Chaos.**" Then we often suck others into our emotional turmoil, hoping they'll rescue us in some way (a form of a victim mindset). When we are in this cycle of chaos, we'll either repel Mr. Right or attract Mr. Wrong as I did in my first marriage. Neither is a desirable option.

A colossal mistake women make on a date is to unload their life chaos onto Mr. Potential. I've noticed a familiar pattern where women reveal too much early on in dating, like on the first date. It could be anything from sharing about childhood traumas, bad exes, trouble with the children, financial issues, etc. Please don't ask me how I know this!

THE SUPERMAN ENCOUNTER

At one point in my journey, I worked at a TV production studio. The owner of a production company rented one of our editing suites for his clients. He was the Superman doppelgänger, with shiny black hair and piercing blue eyes. Did I mention he was also tall and muscular, kind, funny, and generous? It was challenging to keep my composure around him.

He threw out subtle hints of interest in me, and I would subtly respond in kind. I let him take the lead, and then he asked me out. I was so excited about our first date.

I got my hair, nails, and make-up done and bought a cute new outfit. When he showed up at the door, I looked hot. His eyes gleamed with appreciation, and you could feel the connection between us. He took me to a beautiful, posh restaurant where we had a great conversation and a fantastic synergy, and everything was going perfectly. He made me feel so comfortable as if I could share anything. That's when it happened. Yep, I made the colossal chaos mistake.

I unloaded with verbal diarrhea and began sharing about the ordeal with my ex-husband, the hurts of the marriage, and my challenges and tribulations. The list went on.

It was like the music came to a screeching halt, and his eyes glazed over from the intensity of my chaos. I was clueless about what was happening and continued to unload. He began looking at his watch and then waited for the moment he could politely let me know that he had to leave. His excuse was that he had to get up early for a video shoot.

After that, his "interest door" slammed shut. We were back to "friend and client." He was his nice, funny self, but his attraction to me was over. I felt rejected and couldn't understand what had happened.

The men we meet on the journey to "the one" can be the most valuable teachers if we let them. I'm grateful for these men that God used to teach me things about myself that needed to change.

As fate would have it, a couple of years went by after my disastrous dinner date with the production owner, and I saw him at a coffee shop. He immediately recognized me and came to my table to say hello. He asked if he could sit down. We caught up with what had been happening in our lives.

Then, the moment came when there was a pause in our conversation as we looked at each other. I seized the moment and practiced tremendous courage. Taking a deep breath, I said, "Can I ask you a question?"

He looked at me intently and said, "Yes."

I asked, "What caused you to lose interest after our first dinner date?"

He paused and gently said, "I had a great connection with you, but I was overwhelmed. My head started spinning when you started talking about all the chaos in your life. You shared about all the hurt and pain from your ex and a lot of other negative things. It was too much for me, and I backed off."

Can you say "OUCH!?" I had repelled a great guy. As painful as it was to hear his words, it was a pivotal moment of truth in my life. I could have chosen to be offended or beat myself up for blowing it. Instead, I chose to give myself grace and learn from what had happened.

After that encounter, I realized that he had not rejected *me;* he had rejected the *behaviors* I was operating in. When we feel rejected, it's easy to fall into the trap of thinking we aren't enough. We aren't pretty enough, smart enough, skinny enough, or fill-in-the-blank enough.

Unloading all my traumas and overwhelming him is what caused him to shut the door. When I realized I had made the mistake of sharing too much too soon, I gave myself permission to learn from this and space to grow. It was also an opportunity to do a deeper dive and ask myself what would make me feel the need to unload my chaos onto him.

After thinking about that question, it became clear that after dumping my chaos onto him, I was looking for someone to "rescue" me. It was about how he could fulfill the unresolved things in my soul. A part of me was subconsciously still in the *WIIFM* victim mindset. If someone rescued me, I wouldn't have to take responsibility for the cycle of chaos. In essence, I was again trying to fill a void within me that no man can fill except my heavenly Creator.

THE DRAMA ADDICTION

Awareness is the key to change. As I became aware of the various areas of my life that needed change, I noticed others who were operating as chaos queens. They were making the same mistakes I made with good men.

We'll call this woman "Diane," who is another wonderful woman I met on my journey. She was charismatic, savvy, funny, and an incredible speaker who could capture an audience like no other. She had been single for over two decades but had no problem attracting good Mr. Potentials. The challenge was that Mr. Potentials would suddenly disappear, and she couldn't figure out why.

In getting to know her, I realized she was addicted to drama. She thrived on the attention and sympathy of others it created. She had a constant, swirling tornado of stress around her, drawing others into her chaotic world. She was the queen of chaos. When she walked into the room, she emitted a state of chaotic energy.

On her dates, Mr. Potential would have to listen to the stories about how someone died, the weather was bad, someone else was sick in the hospital, and the ex was trying to sabotage her relationship with the kids with his wicked girlfriend. Her friend slept with her other friend's husband, and so forth. It was the never-ending drama train, and she effectively repelled each good guy. Clueless, she continued the pattern in her life as successful as she was. Was she open to input? No.

There are many reasons we may be engaging in constant chaos. It's important to examine the emotional root, attention benefits, or belief systems that cause us to be in this continuous state.

It's normal to need counsel, comfort, or an ear to listen as you process your truth. However, this is best done with friends, counselors, etc., and NOT with Mr. Potential.

A healthy man isn't going to be attracted to a woman who's in a constant state of drama and chaotic energy.

POOR NEGATIVE NELLIE

Let's look at a woman we'll call "negative Nellie." In this season of her life, she was a widow who had raised four children. She was attractive, strong, good-hearted, and constantly helping other people. She really wanted a husband and was getting depressed about being single for so long. There was a pattern of meeting Mr. Potential, having what seemed like a great connection, but then he would suddenly disappear.

What she didn't realize was that every day, she was complaining about something or someone, and there was always an emergency of some kind. The car broke down again, and the water pipe in the house broke and flooded the floor. The dog was sick, the mailman was rude to her, etc.

Negative Nellie would complain about what her kids did or didn't do, about her coffee not served hot enough, about her food at the restaurant, and about the weather. If there were three clouds in the sky, she would see it as dreary and overcast instead of a blue sky with billowy clouds.

She would complain about not having enough money to pay her bills because she gave her money to others in need. The stress was affecting her health, and she would complain about it regularly. She was in a constant state of stress but loved the attention. Inside, she had a lack of identity and a deep-seated need for validation.

Being that Nellie was such a *do-gooder* who always helped everyone, her friends enabled her behavior by feeling sorry for her. *Oh, poor Nellie, she's always having something bad happening but is always helping others.* Negative Nellie thrived on the attention and the chaos. When it came to men, she was repelling them faster than a flash of lightning. Do you see a pattern from these examples?

Let's do a quick evaluation of your "conversation awareness." Reflect and think about the common themes in your conversations listed on the next page. Do you find yourself engaging in any form of these "Queen of Chaos" behaviors? Awareness is the first step to freedom. Give yourself grace.

♥ Check the behaviors below that apply to you (even if in varying forms):

— Do you consistently talk about negative things? Like about who died, who's sick, who got divorced, whose spouse cheated, or how bad the weather is, etc.?

— Do you consistently talk about health problems or financial problems that draw negative attention to yourself? Do you gossip about your co-workers and family members or complain about all your problems and so forth?

— Do you complain about friends who disappointed you, or how so and so did this or that?

— Do you always have a sad, negative story to share?

— Are you subconsciously looking for someone to rescue you?

— Deep down, do you need/enjoy the attention that all the negative stories bring?

— Does complaining draw sympathy from others?

♥ Is there a consistent theme in your responses above? Jot your thoughts below.

_____

_____

_____

_____

_____

_____

_____

_____

♥ Next, honestly evaluate your previous dates with the questions in mind that we just went over. Did you share too much too soon? What did the conversations from your end revolve around? Was the conversation all about you? Did you unload with verbal diarrhea like I did?

_____

_____

_____

_____

_____

_____

♥ Journal your insights as you meditate on these questions.

_____

_____

_____

_____

_____

_____

_____

_____

_____

If you say, "Yes. I've been operating in varying forms of the Queen of Chaos," then congratulations! You are on the right track to positively change your romance results! You are on the path to becoming the royal queen who stops repelling good men.

HOMEWORK ASSIGNMENT:

Are you ready for the mindset challenge? For the next three days, I want you to complete the following exercises:

- ♥ Become aware and notice how many negative thoughts go through your mind. Jot it down.

_____

_____

_____

_____

_____

_____

_____

- ♥ Refrain from telling one negative story, thing, or complaint to anyone. Write each negative thought or something you said during this exercise. This will help you recognize what your mind defaults to.

_____

_____

_____

_____

_____

_____

_____

♥ What was your experience doing this? Was it easy or hard? Did you complain about having to do these exercises? How often did you find yourself in a negative thought, comment, or complaint?

_____

_____

_____

_____

_____

_____

_____

♥ When talking with people for the next three days, tell them one thing you are thankful for, say something positive, give them a compliment, or share one uplifting story. It could be something as simple as finding your favorite nail polish or finding a parking spot right away. For example, a positive observation could be admiring the beautiful clouds in the sky today. If you don't have an uplifting story, search for a miracle story on YouTube.

♥ Journal how people responded to you when you only spoke about positive things. What were their facial expressions and comments? How do you feel about sharing positive experiences?

_____

_____

_____

_____

_____

_____

_____

POSITIVE DECLARATIONS

The key is to begin to train your brain to be grateful and positive and break the negative talk. **Speak positive declarations in the morning, afternoon, and night.** Put one hand on your heart (skin to skin). Place your other hand in a receiving mode, and with a fiery passion from your belly, speak the following:

- ♥ I give myself permission to change!
- ♥ I release myself from all drama and chaos. I accept peace and joy!
- ♥ Things come easy for me!
- ♥ The solutions will present themselves to me!
- ♥ I attract and receive blessings in my life!

If other positive affirmations come to mind, jot them down below and include them in your daily routine.

_____

_____

_____

_____

_____

_____

_____

_____

The more you practice these principles, the more you will attract not only blessings but also Mr. Right.

Reflections FROM JOANNA

You are doing this!

Congratulations! You go girl!

Let's go over the highlights of the chapter. It's important to recognize where we're locked in the chaos cycle. Freedom comes with identifying the emotional root behind it. For example, are we wanting sympathy and attention, or have an unmet need for where we're seeking compassion?

We also want to recognize our negativity and complaining. Next, make optimistic declarations, talk about great things, share uplifting anecdotes. Season your conversations with positivity and watch how others respond to you.

In the next chapter we are going to look at how our director and fixer skills can inadvertently attract Mr. Wrong and repel Mr. Right.

As women, we have a unique ability to multi-task and direct at the same time. It could be disciplining the kids while cooking, feeding the dog while chatting on the phone with our girlfriend. All the same time! We are excellent directors and fixers.

We are going to look at how we can get in trouble with these skills and also known as the back seat driver.

Are you ready for more? Let's do it!

Chapter Seven
THE DIRECTOR
(AKA The Backseat Driver)

Mistake #5

> *God made Adam first because He didn't want any unsolicited advice from Eve!*
>
> UNKNOWN AUTHOR

What a very funny and poignant quote! However, how often do we women offer unsolicited advice, instruction, or information no one asks for?

We have amazing intuition and inner knowing skills. As a result, we are right about things and can feel unheard when our man ignores our input. We excel at identifying ways to improve things. We often point out what our man is doing wrong and how to do it differently. Where we get into trouble and repel a good man is when these skills take on the role of **"The Director."**

What is The Director, you might wonder? I'm glad you asked. The Director is also referred to as the **"Back Seat Driver."** She likes to be in control because she knows best, offers unsolicited advice, and gives input on how something should be done her way. She is also the first to let you know what you did incorrectly. The Director is very good at organizing other people's lives, inadvertently avoiding her own issues.

Often, Director behaviors are rooted out of a deep-seated need to control. The need to control can be rooted in a subconscious fear of something. Most of the time, we aren't aware we're operating in this realm. As a result, we engage in superhero deactivator behaviors that cause a man to feel demeaned, stupid, and incompetent. The very opposite of how we want to make him feel.

> **Remember, good men want to be your superhero and want to feel appreciated. Yet it's easy to forget that men are wired differently than women. We can get stuck in our mental matrix of thinking their needs are not as important as ours. *WIIFM***

The need to direct and help others is often rooted in a deeper need for self-validation to stave off feelings of unworthiness. It can also be a form of a self-protection mechanism to avoid dealing with past hurt or to take responsibility for choices.

> **What comes out of our mouths dictates our outcomes and creates our worlds.**

A different variation of the Director is one who chooses "Man-Projects." Having a man-project makes her feel good because she is bettering someone else (Mr. Potential). It may give her a false sense of purpose and fulfill a need to be needed. The song by Lobo, *I'd Love You to Want Me,* comes to mind.

Typically, one reason we try to change someone is because we need to make changes within ourselves. However, we are often unwilling to make inner changes. Then, we project those needs onto others. That was me at one time. Other times, the person does need to make changes, but that's when we should step away and not be their savior (The Rescuer).

We may also try to change a guy because of a deep-seated fear of getting hurt. Having a "man-project" can make us feel in control and give us a sense of superiority because he needs "our help." It shields us from pain and vulnerability because we know he's not all we truly desire. Therefore, it eliminates the risk of being rejected by the man we would really want to have. Dating Mr. Potential is safe for us but totally unfair to him. It is another form of *WIIFM* (What's In It For Me?).

If you control the relationship, you won't get hurt, right? Wrong! You repel the good men and emotionally damage the man-project. It ultimately keeps you single or compromised in an unhappy marriage.

Have you ever picked a man-project or tried to control Mr. Potential? Some examples of man-project behaviors would be that you drive long distances to see him, but he doesn't do that for you. Or you direct him to rehab, clean up his credit, and give him money while he gets his degree. Because of what you did for him, he has become this or accomplished that.

It's all about what **you** did, and the man-project's life is much better because of **you**. In a way, he now **"owes" you** because **you "helped"** him, which feeds your need to be in control. Perhaps you continually remind him how you helped him, which inadvertently makes him feel demeaned and emasculated as a man. These behaviors often drive men to seek validation from someone else (not you) who "will appreciate him." How often have we heard that?

BOSS BETTY

Let's take a quick look at a woman we'll call "Betty." She was in her sixties and had been married for 35 years. One day, out of the blue, her husband said he was divorcing her and confessed there was another woman. Naturally, Betty was devastated. She was clueless as to how her husband could "suddenly" do this to her.

After all, she had put him through medical school and supported him financially so he could build his practice. She ran the front office like clockwork. All her friends told her what a sacrificial and good wife she was.

There are two sides to every marriage, and both spouses contribute in some way to the failure of a marriage. In this scenario, we are looking at what Betty did to contribute to the deterioration of her relationship.

In doing a deep dive, she was inadvertently making her husband feel inferior and demeaned. She had a deep-seated inner need to be validated and affirmed for her good works. As a result, she constantly reminded her husband how she made him the man he was. She was the reason for his success. Her sacrifices are what has brought them to this point. Is this true? Yes, in part.

However, over time, her words continued to tear him down, make him feel like he owed her, demean him, and make him think he was less than her. It was a way for her to control him. These behaviors and words are superhero deactivators.

Yes, she contributed to their success, but so did he. They did it together, and she didn't acknowledge his hard work. He's the one that had to make it through med school and graduate. He's the one that had to work on his patients and provide them with the best care. Good bedside manners were necessary for him to retain patients. He helped build the practice just as much as she did, but she didn't acknowledge his contribution. It was all about her.

Can you see how her actions contributed to the demise of the marriage and why he suddenly wanted a divorce after 35 years of this kind of treatment? The other woman validated him, encouraged him, and appreciated his hard work. The sad thing is Betty didn't realize what she was doing. She didn't have the awareness during the marriage to recognize her behaviors and make changes before it was too late.

I played various forms of The Director role like Betty and often chose man-projects. Looking back at my inner motivations, choosing a man-project was a way for me to feel in control **because he "needed" me**. It masked my deep-seated fear of getting hurt. At that time, deep down, the thought of meeting a great guy scared me. I was afraid of giving my heart to someone great and then getting rejected by him.

If I met someone who was my potential Mr. Right, a part of me didn't feel worthy enough. I didn't know my true value at the time and was self-sabotaging by gravitating toward men I had to "rescue."

Does any of this resonate with you? Don't worry; you're not the only one. **Being the director of a man-project was safe because, ultimately, he wasn't what I was really looking for. He had potential, and with *my help*, he could be molded to be what I wanted. It was a clear case of *WIIFM*** My mindset was *I'm going to save him and then make him perfect for me.* It fed my ego. My identity was rooted in playing the Savior, which was ultimately the Back Seat Driver.

After being divorced for several years, I met a nice guy named Derek. However, in my eyes, he needed a little fixing. He became my Man-Project.

As we were getting to know each other, I would *direct him* with suggestions on how he could improve himself. I offered unsolicited advice by recommending self-help books and researching good therapists he could choose from. Oh yes, I was the all-knowing one. When he made mistakes, I was quick to point out what he did wrong and let him know how stupid that was.

I also utilized my administrative skills and created menus designed to help him lose the muffin top. I bought him different styles of clothes I knew would look better. What was in his closet was frumpy. In my supreme wisdom, I even offered suggestions on fat-burning workout routines. In addition, there was a great special at the gym he should join.

Does this sound familiar? Do you pick man-projects? Do you try to change a guy? Do you offer your *expert opinions* on things he needs to change in his life or that of others?

To my surprise, these recommendations didn't sit well with Derek. He finally exploded one day because he couldn't take one more bit of advice and said to me in a loud, irritated tone, "Why are we always talking about what I need to fix about myself? Why don't we talk about what YOU need to change? Why can't you accept me for who I am?

What if I said to you that you need to lose weight, fix the wrinkles on your face, and buy nicer clothes? How would you feel if I told you to stop stuffing your face with cookies and ice cream, get rid of your muffin top, and go work out? Why are you even dating me?"

Silence filled the air as I stared at him in shock and didn't know what to say. OUCH! He was right!

I didn't accept him for who he was and didn't affirm the good qualities about him. I focused on what was "wrong," making him feel unattractive, fat, nitpicked, and criticized. Was I doing that on purpose? No, not at all. In my mental matrix, I was "helping" him to better himself. I was the backseat driver and the man-breaker.

How we do anything is how we do everything. How many people have we unknowingly made to feel this way?

Derek demonstrated tremendous emotional courage to stop and challenge my controlling behaviors. I am thankful he said something. If I was un-coachable, I could have responded in offense to him. I could have exploded with how unappreciative he was after everything I had done *for* him!

Fortunately, I had learned to be coachable. After I realized how I had hurt his feelings, I took full responsibility and apologized. He was right. I affirmed all the positive things about him and thanked him for his courage to speak up and say something. He thanked me for listening to him and forgave me. We decided to remain friends and are still good friends to this day.

> **The men we meet on the journey to Mr. Right are the best teachers if we let them.**

Let's look at a little more extreme example of the director. There was a woman we'll call "Louise." She asked her boyfriend, William, to move in with her. She committed to "help" support him through law school. He offered to pay her money for rent, food, bills, etc., but she declined. She wanted to support him and help him stay focused on school.

Louise had a job that paid well, and she could afford all the expenses on her own. She *wanted* to pay all the bills and control the finances. Controlling the finances and having him under her dominion gave her a sense of control and importance. She made him feel indebted to and dependent on her. Ultimately, this made it harder for him to leave.

As a result, she would tell him *what* needed to be done, *when* it needed to be done, and *how* it should be done. She directed most aspects of his life. If he bought groceries with his money, she would get upset and rag on him about purchasing the wrong items.

She was proud of the fact that she was making all the sacrifices (The Martyr Syndrome). Then she would complain to her friends that he didn't seem to appreciate her and took her for granted. Her friends would gush at what a do-gooder she was to help her boyfriend so much. They praised her *kind-heartedness* and how much she loved him. The social accolades were her *WIIFM*

At home, she constantly held it over his head about how she was making all the money and made him feel totally diminished. I knew him. He was a hard worker, very nice, and good husband material. What do you think was the outcome of this relationship?

The day came when he couldn't take her controlling and demeaning behaviors anymore. Halfway through law school, he left her like a flash of lightning. Naturally, she blamed him. She was offended and accused him of using her after everything she did for him. She told all her friends, *"I'm so hurt after everything I did for him! I can't believe he left me. All he wanted was my money!"* And the list went on. It took him a while to get healed from the damage of her controlling and demeaning behaviors.

Louise was a man-breaker. But it never occurred to her that she played a major role in Derek leaving because of the way she treated him. She repelled him. In addition, she was unteachable and wouldn't take responsibility for her part in the breakup.

Did she make him feel like a superhero? No! She wouldn't allow him to share the financial burden each time he offered. She tried to control everything he did. She held her "generosity" over his head. Not only that, but she also rejected him. She rejected his efforts to help; she rejected who he was as a man, and she rejected his good heart.

What could Louise have done differently with Derek? For starters, she shouldn't have invited him to move in. It would have been better to allow him his own independence. However, being that she did, she could have allowed him to contribute to the financial responsibilities as he wanted. He wasn't a lazy bum trying to mooch off her. She also could have acknowledged and thanked him for the contributions he was making. She could have affirmed his hard work.

Going to law school is no easy feat. She could have made him feel like a superhero by complementing the fabulous job he was doing managing everything. She could have affirmed and thanked him for the things he did, like buying the groceries, taking out the trash, etc. He did a lot of other things.

Do you see how Louise's relationship could have been great and led to a marriage with a good man? Instead, she needed to have all the attention (good or bad), which was ultimately rooted in fear, insecurity, the need to dominate, control, and selfishness. (*WIIFM*)

Remember, we women are the queens on the chessboard. We have the influence of being a man-breaker or a kingmaker. Which one are you?

If you find yourself operating in various forms of the director, it's time to stop and re-evaluate yourself. Ask yourself, "Why do I feel the need to control? Why do I need to play the role of the martyr or the Do-Gooder? What are my social or emotional payoff for these behaviors?" Attention? Validation of your self-esteem? Ego?

These are tough questions, but necessary. If you have operated in these tendencies, now is the perfect time to stop, meditate, and reflect on your previous relationships and behaviors. Don't condemn yourself, but honestly evaluate yourself. Do you operate in these behaviors with men, friends, family, children, or co-workers?

Remember, freedom begins with the willingness to take responsibility for our choices. It comes from the willingness to humble ourselves and take action to change. Doing so allows us to grow like a flower and experience better outcomes in our lives, especially in the arena of our romantic results.

PRACTICAL APPLICATION

Let's conduct a quick, honest inventory of the inner you. On a scale of 1 (low) to 10 (highest), how would you honestly rate your need to direct and backseat drive?

1   2   3   4   5   6   7   8   9   10   (*Circle One*)

♥ Do you do what I did by offering unsolicited advice or counsel on what needs to be changed in a man or others? List two recent examples of where you've done this.

_____

_____

_____

_____

_____

_____

_____

_____

♥ Do you gravitate toward Man-Projects? What kinds of things are you doing for your Man-Project? For example, are you supporting him, being his emotional coach, paying for his gas, groceries, bills, coaching, etc.? What is the emotional payoff from doing this?

_____

_____

_____

_____

_____

_____

♥ When you find yourself engaging in various rescuing tendencies, what part of you is seeking attention? What aspect of your identity requires validation from others to prove your worthiness as a person? Are you afraid of rejection in some way? What part of you needs healing?

_____

_____

_____

_____

_____

_____

_____

_____

♥ If you're honest, what in you causes the need to control, offer unsolicited advice, direct, or point out what's wrong? Where does this stem from?

_____

_____

_____

_____

_____

_____

_____

_____

I'm really proud of you for being willing to take an honest inventory of yourself! There's no shame, only gain! These upcoming steps are crucial in reversing the role of The Director. You will want to journal your responses.

HOMEWORK ASSIGNMENT:

♥ Acknowledge and take responsibility where you are the Director. In what areas of your life is this relevant?

_____

_____

_____

_____

_____

_____

_____

_____

♥ **Be willing to apologize as appropriate.** What mistakes have you made with someone else? Make a list of individuals to whom you owe an apology.

_____

_____

_____

_____

_____

_____

_____

♥ **Become aware of deeper fears, insecurities, and feelings of unworthiness within yourself.** What are they? What's the root? Remember to give yourself grace.

_____

_____

_____

_____

_____

_____

AWARENESS EXERCISE

♥ For the next three days, apply what I call "spiritual duct tape" to your mouth and start intentionally recognizing and stopping yourself from giving anyone unsolicited advice, correction, or instruction. How many times did you catch yourself? What type of situation occurred?

_____

_____

_____

_____

_____

_____

_____

♥ **Acknowledge your Man-Projects and let them go immediately.**
I always permit myself to change my mind given new information. Having this mindset has changed my life because I was willing to see things from a unique perspective. Being coachable will get you far in life!

The path of truth is lighting up before you! You are getting through the exercises like a champ! I'm so proud of your willingness and courage to acknowledge areas in your life that need adjusting. What's interesting is the definition of "repent" means to **change your mind**.

Great job so far!

Reflections FROM JOANNA

Congratulations! We are getting there!

Remember, good men want to be your superhero and want to feel appreciated. They want to impress you.

We became aware of the superhero deactivator behaviors such as the need to boss our man, offer unsolicited advice, or dictate how things should be done.

These behaviors make a man feel demeaned, diminished, and stupid. The opposite of how we want someone feel.

We also want to let go of any man-projects in our lives and/or recognize the savior complex within ourselves.

The great news is, now you can identify these behaviors and have learned how to make changes to be the kingmaker!

Do you find yourself competing with men in different ways? If so, read on. If not, keep reading for awareness of what **not** to do.

In the next chapter we are going to explore what appears to be a harmless behavior but will repel a guy faster than a speeding bullet.

Are you ready for more? Let's do it!

Chapter Eight
THE ONE-UPPER
(AKA The Competitor)

Mistake #6

> *Women get the last word in every argument. Anything a man*
> *says after that is the beginning of a new argument!*
>
> UNKNOWN AUTHOR

nd then, men end the conversation with, "Yes, dear!" All joking aside, we're going to unpack the various forms of one-upping connected to this quote and how it repels a good man. Before we do, let's start with a few questions to think about.

Do you find yourself one-upping a guy, whether it be money, wit, or intelligence? Would you say you're typically correct? As a successful career woman or athlete, do you compete with Mr. Potential? Do you have an underlying need to prove yourself?

Certain careers demand women to be strong, edgy, and competitive to earn respect from men. For example, to be a competitive athlete, you must possess a mindset focused on winning and be fully committed. As a business owner, you have to manage employees and navigate the corporate ladder. As a mother, you are the all-knowing one managing a household, job, and family.

However, let's look at some behaviors of the **"One-Upper,"** AKA "the Competitor," when they are out of balance. A One-Upper typically needs the last word. She needs to be right almost all the time, or she may reject others' opinions as inferior. She may argue and WEAR her man down until he says, "Yes, dear."

She may find it challenging to apologize or lack the ability to accept him for who he is. A one-upper may consistently compare her wins and successes to his. She may find it difficult to allow him to do something for her, such as carrying her boxes or pulling out the chair, because she can do it herself better.

A woman may become a Competitor because of subconscious feelings of unworthiness, inferiority, or the need to prove herself.

The Competitor may have had to be "the tough chick" to survive a tough home life, face challenges at school, or climb up the success ladder in a man's world. Maybe mom or dad had perfectionism syndrome, and no matter how hard she tried, it wasn't good enough. Maybe either parent had alcoholism. As a result, this competitive drive becomes a part of her identity or a protection mechanism that covers up the vulnerability of her heart. Is any of this ringing a bell for you?

In my tomboy phase as a little girl, I used to compete with the boys, race them on my bikes, one-up them, and I had to be superior to prove myself. I would get into fights with them. I was the tough chic and would name and shame the boys. It became an identity for me and a subconscious protection mechanism.

Anything you can do, I can do better was my mindset as the One-Upper. These mindsets inadvertently carried themselves into my adulthood. As a successful woman who made her own money, bought her own cars, etc., it was easy to fall into the competition trap with men. I always had to be right or have the last word.

When it came to dating and making a man feel special, it took me a while to figure out that my one-upmanship with Mr. Potential was repelling him. I didn't make him feel special, respected, or honored. I also rejected him because I was rejecting his ideas, thoughts, and feelings.

For example, if he had an opinion about something and I felt he was wrong, I would argue and debate my point until he would go silent. This is a variation of

WIIFM It was all about my feelings, my opinions, and I didn't care what he thought. I was right. In my mind, he was inferior to me. Ego.

Did you know that according to *Men's Health* magazine, a report done by the Jo Cox Commission in 2017 showed that eight million men feel lonely every week? It's a big factor that drives them to porn. Porn can pose as a distraction from their real feelings of depression, rejection from women, loneliness, or lack of confidence. This is not excusing that kind of behavior. It's a statistic that gives a different insight into the inner emotional world of a man.

Remember, the root cause of any addiction is the deep-seated need for love. It's looking for love in all the wrong places and frequently an unwillingness to address the real pain.

I'm sharing this information to provide a better understanding of how our words can affect a man's self-esteem. Often, we women think men are like armor and don't feel any of the effects of our actions or words. I did.

How does it make you feel when someone always has to be correct, argues with you about most things, doesn't apologize, points out your mistakes, and makes you feel dumb? How often do we unknowingly do this to men?

THE UGLY DATING TRUTH

As previously mentioned, I interviewed different men for this book and brought up the subject of what's often referred to as a "one-night stand" or a "hump and dump." Some men shared that when a woman consistently makes a guy feel inferior, demeaned, and unable to measure up, he needs to think that he can do something right. As a result, he sleeps with her, and then she never hears from him again. In his mind, at least he can do something right and have a "win" by getting her into bed.

She may think she got *victory* over him and *used* him for sex. The bottom line is she was used like a rag towel and thrown away. She's still alone, single, and discarded after her one-night stand. Is this right? No.

Nobody wins in these scenarios. She demeans and disrespects him, and he, in turn, uses her and then drops her like a hot potato. He then moves on to a woman who will respect him. Clearly, this is not a healthy dynamic, but how often does this happen?

On the flip side, The Competitor may use her one-upmanship to control a guy. Many women don't realize this type of unhealthy competition is a form of emotional abuse projected onto the man. It's a man-breaking behavior.

Remember: We are talking about the woman's side of the coin in a relationship. My friend, we'll call "Joe," once dated a woman who was The Competitor. We'll call her "Nancy." She was very good at one-upping and pointing out what he could have done better. For example, if he bought Nancy a pretty flower bouquet, she would comment on how those weren't her favorite colors.

When he gave her a thoughtful card, she would complain that he didn't write enough. Nancy refused to acknowledge that he went to the store, spent several minutes picking out the card and then took time to write in it.

She always had a subtle dig, or a complaint about everything Joe tried to do for her. It was never good enough. When he took her to a 5-star restaurant, she would note that the menu wasn't that great, or the food wasn't cooked right. She even told him that every bad thing that happened in her life was his fault. Did this relationship work out? Uh, no.

I have another friend we'll call "John" who was on a date with a woman he thought was his dream girl. We'll call her "Ms. Wrong." John owned a jewelry store and had an eye for high-end pieces. He took her to an elegant, romantic restaurant. During dinner, he was admiring her necklace, but before he could compliment her necklace, she caught his eye.

Suddenly, she started manically waving her hands up and down, repeatedly pointing to her breasts and then up to her face. In a loud, denigrating tone, she said, "Hey! Up here! You can talk to my face!" Her actions startled the people at the other tables, causing them to stop and stare at them.

He felt mortified, humiliated, and utterly shocked by her behavior. He truly was looking at her necklace. Speechless, he sat and stared as her eyes gleamed with a smug look on her face. In her mind, she clearly put him in his place, in public, no less! Ha!

Thankfully, he never went out with her after that, but he was now mistrustful of women. He was afraid of being humiliated, misjudged, and demeaned again.

This is a prime example of what I shared earlier in the chapter about how other women can damage our future men with man-breaking behaviors. How are you treating the men you meet on your journey? How are you handling their mistakes or imperfections?

THE ANTI-DEFENSIVE APPROACH

How do you handle conflict with your man? What is your approach to dealing with a mistake he made? In general, women tend to point something out in an accusatory tone, such as, "You did blah blah" or "You should have done blah blah." I made this classic mistake over and over. It puts a man on the defensive. We want to do the opposite, which is why I call it the anti-defensive technique.

Any time you start a conversation with anyone with the words "YOU did . . ." then the other person is immediately put on the defensive. The anti-defensive tactic removes the word "You" from the vocabulary when confronting.

Instead of assuming the worst and that he intentionally did something, assume the best. Assume that he didn't realize what he did, and speak to him from that perspective.

If it's something that really irritated you or made you angry, work out your feelings first. Then, have a conversation afterward. In addition, make sure it's done privately and never publicly.

For example, instead of starting with "You did . . ." start with "I don't know if you realized or are aware of . . .." Now, you aren't putting him on the defensive in an accusatory tone.

When my husband David and I were dating, I had an opportunity to practice my anti-defensive technique. One day, while we were talking on the phone, David asked me to hold while he took another call. However, he never got back to me, and I was placed on eternal hold.

When this happened twice in a row, I was quite irritated and knew it needed to be addressed. First, I had to process my irritation so that my tone wasn't accusatory when I spoke to him. I addressed it in our next conversation after we had small talk, and we were both in a good emotional space. Timing is everything!

Joanna: "I know you're very busy, and being on the phone is a part of the ministry and business. I understand if you need to get off the phone while we're in the middle of a conversation. Could you do me a favor?"

David: "Sure, what is it?"

Joanna: "Next time we're on a call, and you need to hop off, can you let me know you have to take this call? In the last two conversations, I was placed on an eternal hold, thinking you were going to finish our conversation. I waited for at least five minutes before I finally hung up and felt disrespected. I know you would never intentionally disrespect me or dishonor my time."

David: [Pause]."You're right. I would never intentionally disrespect your time, and I'm sorry. I assumed you knew I had to take the call because it had to do with an immediate prayer need from someone. Next time, I'll let you know when I have to get off the phone."

Do you notice **HOW** I spoke to him about what happened and **HOW** he responded? It had a great outcome because of my approach.

What if I took the accusatory approach of, *"You are so rude, leaving me on hold all the time? I can't believe you did that. You better not do that again!"*

He would have been put on the defensive and offended because I incorrectly *assumed* he was being intentionally rude. It was quite the opposite. He didn't realize what he was doing. In this situation, snarky behavior from me would have been a red flag for him to cut off the relationship. One more reminder: **Little keys unlock big doors and big doors swing on small hinges.**

HIS TWO LEFT FEET

We've addressed making it an intention to leave someone feeling blessed or encouraged in their interaction with you. Now, let's look at this example of how I did this when the guy made a mistake.

This door of opportunity opened during a ballroom dance lesson. I used to do ballroom dancing and became a seasoned dancer. In class, some guys had two left feet, but they were trying to learn.

In one fateful class, I was dancing with Greg, who definitely had two left feet and was very nervous about dancing. While spinning me, he missed catching my hand, and I spun into a pole! After making another round across the dance floor, he accidentally backed me into the same pole. Can you say "OUCH!?" Then, he inadvertently drove me back into the pole a second time.

The old response would have been, "Are you blind? How could you NOT see that pole you just backed me into for a second time?" So, how did I handle the dance situation? I'm glad you asked!

The first time he accidentally spun me into the pole, he immediately apologized, and I told him it was ok. During the second round of dancing, he accidentally backed me into the same pole and looked very embarrassed. He apologized profusely. The second time he backed me into the pole, there was fear in his eyes as he waited for me to unleash (rightfully so). I paused, looked him in the eyes, smiled, and jokingly said, "That pole has it out for me today. You've done a great job with some of those other moves we did."

I will never forget the look on his face. He was shocked and relieved at the same time by my response. He felt encouraged to keep trying. He smiled and then did so much better, and we ended up having a great time.

Imagine if my response had been the old *WIIFM*. How much more humiliated and rejected would he have felt? Most likely, he would never have come back to the dance lessons. A negative reaction from me could have scarred him for the woman he was supposed to be with.

Remember, in chess, the queen protects the king.

If you operate in various forms of The Competitor, now is the time to self-reflect and evaluate yourself. Remember, there is no shame. We can't become a better version of ourselves if we aren't aware. If we don't know what needs to be adjusted, we can't practice the courage to change.

PRACTICAL APPLICATION

It takes time to develop new patterns of behavior, but inch by inch, it's a cinch. Becoming aware and being honest with yourself is the key to freedom. Check the boxes that apply to you.

♥ Do you deeply need to prove yourself? What is the reason? What is the origin of this?

_____

_____

_____

_____

_____

_____

_____

♥ Do you find yourself in the one-upper trap? Describe in further detail.

_____

_____

_____

_____

_____

_____

_____

♥ Do your conversations revolve around you? What's the usual focus?

_____

_____

_____

_____

_____

_____

_____

♥ Do you consistently feel the need to have the final say? List a recent example.

_____

_____

_____

_____

_____

_____

_____

♥ Do you find it difficult to apologize? List a recent example.

_____

_____

_____

_____

_____

_____

_____

_____

♥ Do you often wear people down until they see things your way?

_____

_____

_____

_____

_____

_____

_____

♥ Do you engage in forms of "Thank you for the ... *but* ...."
Or "You did do ... but you didn't do ...!" How often do you do this?

_____

_____

_____

_____

_____

_____

_____

♥ Do you feel the need to point out when you're right?

_____

_____

_____

_____

_____

_____

_____

♥ Do you quickly jump to conclusions? Describe what happened.

_____

_____

_____

_____

_____

_____

_____

♥ Do you typically confront situations with an accusatory "You did _blah blah blah?_" How often does this occur?

_____

_____

_____

_____

_____

_____

_____

_____

♥ How do you typically deal with confrontation in a relationship? e.g., Are you afraid to confront, or do you tend to speak in an accusatory or snarky tone?

_____

_____

_____

_____

_____

_____

_____

♥ As you work through these questions, is there a common theme in your responses? What incidents come to mind? What do you notice?

_____

_____

_____

_____

_____

_____

_____

HOMEWORK ASSIGNMENT:

For ONE WEEK, do the following exercises. Then, journal your experiences.

- ♥ Do not try to "one-up" others. Intentionally let people have the last word. Affirm their witty comments or statements. Note their facial expressions when you do this.

- ♥ Find something positive to talk about in every conversation. Refrain from saying one negative thing.

- ♥ Practice the anti-defensive tactic in the mirror. Start with, "I'm not sure if you're aware . . ." instead of "YOU did . . .."

- ♥ When in conversations, and if it is appropriate, ask more questions to gain a deeper understanding of that person.

- ♥ Say "Thank you" to anything nice someone says or does for you and affirm their behavior. Note their facial expressions as you carry out this task.

Learning to be a better affirmer and listener was a gradual process for me. It took time and some humble pie to say I'm sorry. It required practice to stop trying to outdo others and always having to be right. You're doing great, and I'm so proud of you! Keep up the great work!

I encourage you to practice these techniques with your friends and new people you meet. As you continue to practice these new behaviors, people will increasingly find you engaging and admire your positive energy.

Reflections
FROM JOANNA

You should be feeling proud of yourself! You're pressing in to become the enhanced version of you.

Let's summarize some highlights from this chapter. We discussed the importance of learning how to confront with honor and respect instead of accusing and assuming in error.

You've gained an understanding of how damaging our words and responses can be to a man. Remember the statistic at the beginning of the book? Eight million men struggle with loneliness rooted in rejection every week.

You've seen how an unhealthy form of competition with a man damages the relationship and his inner superhero.

Great job! We are in the home stretch!

Are you ready to look at the mistake that can cost a woman years of her life with the wrong man or miss out on being with Mr. Right? It's something so simple yet profound.

Alright, let's get to the last inning before the home run!

Chapter Nine
THE FANTASIZER
(Falling for Fantasy, Not Reality)

Mistake #7

> *"Emotionally inaccessible" is how some describe it.*
> *I refer to it as "a challenge."*
>
> ANONYMOUS

W hat causes some of us to fall for a guy who is emotionally unavailable on some level or married? Why do we spend our time and energy chasing him, trying to win him over? How many of us have met who appeared to be Prince Charming, but he turned out to be Mr. Toad? How often have we found ourselves getting involved with a guy, only to later question what we initially found attractive about him? Why do we do this?

One of the biggest traps I see women make is **"falling for fantasy"** instead of reality. A part of us doesn't want to see the truth. We are unwilling to look at the deeper wells within us. This mindset will block you from attracting Mr. Right. It happened to me, and I know of so many women this has happened to as well.

Falling for fantasy can cause us to waste months and sometimes years of our lives with undesirable outcomes, emotional damage, and baggage. The harsh reality is approximately 3-5% of men will leave their spouse for the other woman. We can get involved with the wrong man and experience a disastrous marriage like I did or miss our happily ever after with Mr. Right.

There are a few key reasons a woman may subconsciously fall for fantasy and not reality:

- ♥ A deep inner part of her feels unworthy and is afraid of getting hurt again. As a result, she *falls* for a guy who doesn't truly capture her heart.
- ♥ She's in love with the idea of being married and needs someone to fill the emptiness within her that only God can fill.
- ♥ Desperation fueled by a deep-seated need to be rescued on some level.
- ♥ Deferred hope (Loneliness and depression from delayed or unfulfilled life dreams).

Deferred hope causes us to make choices that lead to undesirable romance results. It can cause us to compromise. It can make us believe nothing will change based on very real circumstances, especially if we have been single for a long time and wonder why no one seems to want us. As a result, we may make poor, short-term choices that carry long-term consequences.

Deferred hope can cause amazing, highly intelligent, and successful women to have irrational and obsessive behaviors toward a man. It can cause her to chase fantasy, not reality, and miss her real appointments with destiny.

> **We all experience deferred hope in some way, shape, or form at some point in time. The key is to be aware of it and make different choices.**

As you know, when I first met my ex, Mr. Wrong, he appeared to be funny, successful, caring, had a servant's heart, liked to dance, and seemed to be Prince Charming. Yet, in reality, I had chosen a man who had a casual relationship with the truth, was a secret alcoholic, etc. I wasted precious time and energy on this guy and repelled the good guys. Why?

For starters, my subconscious motivations were rooted in *WIIFM*. I was in love with the idea of being a wife and wanted someone to make MY dreams come true. It was all about my needs, and deep down, I struggled with feeling unworthy.

As a result, I allowed myself to get pressured into marriage instead of waiting, which would have resulted in a very different outcome in my life. The good news is that God can turn our mistakes into miracles. If not for Him addressing my myriad of mistakes, I wouldn't be writing this book to help you!

If you are honest with yourself, are you afraid of getting hurt deep down inside, or do you feel unworthy on some level? Are you more in love with the Hollywood concept of the happily ever after than the reality of a healthy relationship? How many good guys have been repelled because, deep down, you really weren't emotionally available?

SOME FALLING FOR FANTASY, NOT REALITY SCENARIOS

Consider "Monica," a sweet, wonderful lady with big hazel eyes who loved everything Italian and had studied abroad in Italy for a year to learn the language. She worked as a programmer for a tech company in Boston, where she met Lorenzo. He was one of the engineers and an authentic Italian.

Naturally, Monica was attracted to him because he embodied her love of romance, and they began dating. They traveled throughout Europe together, and his Italian family instantly loved her. Lorenzo's family owned a beautiful estate and vineyards in the Tuscan area of Italy. They showered Monica with love, gifts, and attention. She loved the attention and his family's love, which met her unrealized need for acceptance. Lorenzo was passionate and intense.

For Monica, this was a beautiful, romantic love story with a happily ever after. Because Monica was so infatuated with the illusion of the Italian romance, she ignored the warning signs of his narcissistic tendencies. She would excuse Lorenzo's emotional intensity as "being a red-hot Italian man."

When he criticized and raised his voice at her, she shrugged it off, thinking *he's just being passionate*. Then he started blaming her for things that went wrong, and he became controlling of the time she should spend with her own family and friends. If she called him out on his behavior, he would accuse her of being the reason for behaving that way. It was all her fault. Monica didn't want to face the reality that her Italian dream come true was turning into a bad dream. Instead, she continued rationalizing his behavior with excuses. She turned a blind eye to all the warning signs.

Against the advice of friends, she married him, and they had three children. As time marched on, his behavior became more and more emotionally abusive, along with his temper. She became the woman under his ruling thumb. Eventually, she found out he was a serial adulterer, and she finally filed for a divorce.

Every woman wants to be loved, wants romance, wants to find her soul mate, and live happily ever after. It's easy to fall in love with the idea of being in love. Being married to the fantasy and unwilling to let go causes us to ignore the warning signs.

If you've been single for a long time, of course, there is a part of you that may feel lonely. Naturally, you don't want to be alone anymore. After getting free of Mr. Wrong, I realized it's better to be alone and lonely than to be married and lonely. Healing of our soul needs to come *before* we meet Mr. Right.

> *"Illusions commend themselves to us because they save us pain and allow us to enjoy pleasure instead. We must, therefore, accept it without complaint when they sometimes collide with a bit of reality against which they are dashed to pieces."*
>
> SIGMUND FREUD, REFLECTIONS ON WAR AND DEATH

The reality is we sometimes don't want to see the truth. We don't want to face the pain of our situation. Falling for fantasy is an avoidance mechanism often rooted in the unwillingness to look at oneself. We blame others and play the victim. In my situation with Mr. Wrong, I was unwilling to look at the truth and ignored my intuition about getting married.

The key to my freedom was asking God to hold up a mirror to my face and help me understand what caused me to make the choices I did. What happened because I gave myself the grace to acknowledge the truth and make changes within myself?

I put in the effort to do the emotional work and develop love and respect for myself. I learned to forgive myself and others. I learned to become a kingmaker. Eventually, I met, married, and have remained happily married to my king.

KAT THE ATTORNEY

Let's look at a different scenario about someone we'll call "Kat." She was a successful, attractive corporate attorney. She had all the money and friends she could want. Yet, at 50 years old, she'd never been married or had any children. One day, she was sitting at a French café when a very well-known public figure walked in. Their eyes met, and she felt an instant connection to this man. He was magnetic.

A conversation ensued, and they decided to connect on social media. Kat never physically saw him after that, and he never asked for her phone number. Nevertheless, within her fantasy, she was completely convinced that this man, boasting 98k followers, had a genuine interest in her. He was sending her coded messages through his public profile. In her justification, the reason he was sending her secret messages was because of his high-profile status. The other women would get jealous if they knew he was interested in her.

If we dig a little deeper into Kat's life, she was raised as an only child and was spoiled growing up. Her parents doted on her, and the world revolved around Kat. Growing up with everything done for her led to an expectation that others should do the same. She was a kind and thoughtful person, not realizing what her modus operandi was. Naturally, she expected Mr. Potential to drop everything to cater to all of her needs. Of course, healthy men were repelled by her self-centered behavior.

Because of the pain of feeling rejected by men, she needed a fantasy to hang onto. Instead of evaluating what she was doing so that she could do better, she became stuck in the single cycle.

THE DISTANT HUSBAND

Meet someone we'll call "Ann." She was a consultant and owned a couple of different businesses. One day, she had a dream that a very high-profile influencer was her future husband. She became friends with his public social media profile and went to several of his events. Ann would often fly out to his state to visit his church. She got to know his staff, who helped manage everything. She believed that getting to know them would provide an opportunity to meet him.

Ann would post on social media about how he was the perfect match for her. She made it sound like they were together and that he was going to take care of her. In her posts, she bragged about being the future "Mrs." so and so.

She even went as far as to move to his state and neighborhood. She rented a house on the same block as if they had a relationship. Ann was sharing her exciting news on social media, yet she still had not met him.

Shockingly, things didn't work out. When it didn't play out the way she predicted, Ann told her social media friends an "evil force" had blocked her from marrying him. What would cause an intelligent and savvy businesswoman to be deceived like this?

A part of her didn't want to be single anymore, and she was unwilling to address the pain of the root cause of her situation. If you were to look into the crystal ball of her life, you would see the superhero deactivator behaviors she engaged in with other men. She was the Shamer, Controller and had an unwillingness to humble herself to understand what needed to change within herself.

In her mind, she was destined to be married to a high-profile man with money. Having a husband like that would bring her prestige and accolades. She could boast about being married to "so and so" and the financial benefits she'd gain. Can you say *WIIFM* It wasn't about how she could help complement his life; her mindset was about **her advantages if she were married to him.**

> *It's not enough to be at the right place at the right time. You have to be the right person in the right place at the right time.*
>
> T. HARVE EKER

If you find yourself relating in various forms to the examples, this is excellent news! Being aware is the #1 key to changing your romance results.

PRACTICAL APPLICATION

♥ The first step is to recognize the fantasy thinking or behaviors. Where have you done this in the past? Is this your current mindset?

_____

_____

_____

_____

_____

_____

_____

_____

Examine and write the answers to the questions below.

♥ Have you ever engaged in falling for fantasy or an emotionally unavailable man? What happened on the date or in the relationship? How did you see yourself at the time?

_____

_____

_____

_____

_____

_____

_____

_____

♥ What caused you to be attracted to this guy? i.e., Did he sweet talk you, romance you, make big promises, etc.? Was his financial status a lure?

_____

_____

_____

_____

_____

_____

_____

_____

♥ Did you have any fantasy beliefs that made you overlook certain behaviors? If so, what were the behaviors you overlooked?

_____

_____

_____

_____

_____

♥ Are you dating someone who displays red flags? If so, what should you do to end this relationship?

_____

_____

_____

_____

_____

_____

_____

If you need to grieve the losses of your mistakes, it's ok to do so, but don't stay in that place. Allow yourself to realize the reality of what you did, forgive yourself, and be thankful for this education that will prepare you for Mr. Right! He's waiting for you!

HOMEWORK ASSIGNMENT:

For one week, speak positive affirmations. Feel free to add your own affirmations. I encourage you to continue speaking the affirmations to yourself and make them a routine. This helps to retrain your brain. The experts say it takes thirty days to change habits.

- ♥ I choose to walk in truth and give myself the grace to see my weaknesses.
- ♥ I am courageous for being willing to humble myself.
- ♥ I attract healthy relationships and my Mr. Right cannot wait to meet me!
- ♥ I am beautiful and special!
- ♥ I love myself!
- ♥ I receive all the blessings heaven sends my way!
- ♥ I let go of all *WIIFM* mindsets!
- ♥ I accept myself!
- ♥ I release all unforgiveness and bitterness!
- ♥ I am successful and joyful, and great things happen for me!

Reflections
FROM JOANNA

I'm so proud of you! GREAT job!

Now it's time to celebrate your hard work! You have earned it! I can't wait to hear the testimonies of great stories you will have to share.

It's time to put to into practice what you've learned. So, let's talk about how to walk out your destiny and recap the principles you have learned.

Here we go . . .

Chapter Ten
YOU DID IT!

Walking Into Your Destiny

> *Mirror, Mirror, looking back at me, tell me what I need to see.*
> *Some days, I gaze and think to myself,*
> *"If I could only be like somebody else."*
> *The mirror replied back to me,*
> *"It's time to see the real beauty you were created to be."*
>
> JOANNA HAIRABEDIAN

ONGRATULATIONS—YOU DID IT! **Take pride in yourself for reading this entire book.** You deserve the best because you possess beauty, strength, and courage. It takes courage to lean in and admit the good, bad, and ugly about yourself and accept/forgive yourself.

Walking into the unknown of change requires courage. It's a choice to say NO to fear and YES to courage and take the steps it takes to do it. You're doing it! And it's **your** time to shine!

Let's review some highlights from each chapter about mistakes that repel good men. We'll recap superhero deactivators and king- or man-breaking behaviors. Then, we will affirm you.

> *Death and life are in the power of the tongue.*
>
> PROVERBS 18:21A KJV

Words create life and build up. Words tear down and bring death. What world are you creating with your words?

CHAPTER 1: WIIFM (WHAT'S IN IT FOR ME?) SYNDROME

The healthy *WIIFM* mindset helps you do good business, maintain healthy boundaries, and have a balanced give-and-take in a relationship. The unhealthy form of *WIIFM* predominately revolves around your needs. How others should take care of you, promote you, fulfill your dreams, rescue you, complete you, etc. For this book, we have addressed the unhealthy *WIIFM* which is the root of all failed relationships.

The healthy *WIIFM* has healthy boundaries, healthy expectations, and a mindset of mutual servanthood. We discussed the Hollywood media stereotypes of men and women that create unhealthy relationship mindsets. Men are portrayed as the "bad boy" abuser, the friend, or the dumb doormat.

Women are portrayed as weak-willed women, sex toys, or dominating nags. It's vital to understand where this media programming has influenced your romance expectations.

CHAPTER 2: THE BEAUTIFUL YOU

Here, we learned there is:

- ♥ Power in agreement.
- ♥ Power in words.
- ♥ Power in receiving a blessing.
- ♥ Power in forgiving yourself.

Words create and build up. Words tear down and destroy. We learned to come out of agreement with the lies about ourselves. Learning to accept and honor ourselves is a cornerstone in attracting a healthy man. You are beautiful inside and out, and it's important to forgive yourself and see yourself with compassion.

CHAPTER 3: THE KINGMAKER AND THE MAN-BREAKER

In the game of chess, the Queen rules the board, and her role is to protect the king. We want to be women who are kingmakers and not man-breakers. Man-breakers publicly and privately shame, demean, criticize, and control men. She typically has an unhealed rage, bitterness, or unforgiveness toward men.

There's always something the guy did that was wrong. She shames him privately and publicly. Kingmakers publicly and privately affirm their man. They receive his compliments and acknowledge and appreciate his efforts. They protect his heart, not tear it apart with words. Remember, the most important opinion to a man is that of his queen.

CHAPTER 4: THE REVERSE TRAINER

When the inability to receive outweighs the ability to give, we are Reverse Trainers. We train people on how to treat us, either good or bad. The reverse trainer is someone who trains others how to stop giving her compliments or gifts. She calls negative attention to herself and inadvertently blocks her blessings in life. She rejects others by rejecting or dismissing their compliments. The reverse trainer has a victim mentality for everything happening to her and doesn't want to take responsibility.

CHAPTER 5: THE DISGUISED DOORMAT, THE YES SYNDROME

The Disguised Doormat is strong and independent and can hold her own until she gets involved with a man. When she gets into a relationship, she loses her identity and moves into "fear of losing him" mode. The disguised doormat gives up her personal power. His world slowly becomes her world.

She develops the Yes Syndrome, where she's the "Yes, I'm available anytime that's convenient for you" type. When it comes to him, she puts her needs aside. She's still successful with everything else, but in the relationship, the disguised doormat becomes the man-pleaser. As a result, Mr. Potential will typically leave if he's an emotionally healthy man. Or she will attract abusers who may mistreat her.

CHAPTER 6: THE QUEEN OF CHAOS

A colossal mistake women make on a date is to unload their life chaos onto Mr. Potential too early in the dating process, especially on the first date. The Queen of Chaos has a constant tornado of swirls about her and loves attention from all the negative things that happen in her life.

Often, it's an excuse not to address the internal issues. The Queen of Chaos thrives on drama and being in a constant state of emergency. She overwhelms the emotionally healthy Mr. Potential, and it causes him to run away.

CHAPTER 7: THE DIRECTOR, AKA THE BACK SEAT DRIVER

The Director is the Back Seat Driver who needs to be in control because she knows best! She offers unsolicited advice, calls people names, and dictates how things need to be done. It's her way; the Director is smarter than everyone else.

The Director is very good at organizing other people's lives, so she avoids addressing her own life. She tends to choose "Man-Projects" because they give her a false sense of purpose and fulfill a need to be needed. The Director can cause a man to feel diminished and hen-pecked.

CHAPTER 8: THE ONE-UPPER, AKA THE COMPETITOR

The One-Upper is a female who competes with a guy in various ways. She has to have the last word, and she needs to be right or prove she's right. She rejects his opinions as inferior. A one-upper may argue with him until he says, "Yes, dear."

One-Uppers also may find it difficult to apologize or lack the ability to accept him for who he is. She may consistently compare her wins and successes with his.

These superhero deactivator behaviors consistently make him feel demeaned, shamed, and less than.

CHAPTER 9: THE FANTASIZER, FALLING FOR FANTASY NOT REALITY

One of the biggest traps a woman makes is falling for fantasy instead of reality. A part of her doesn't want to see the truth. This mindset will block her from attracting Mr. Right. She may do this because a deeper part of her feels unworthy.

When someone is falling for fantasy and not reality, they are in love with the idea of being married, or they want to be rescued in some way. Or she may have deferred hope, which is loneliness and depression from delayed or unfulfilled life dreams.

> **The key to your transformation is giving yourself permission to change your mind given new information.**

Throughout the book, you've practiced courage by taking responsibility for your actions and heart. You're taking the important steps to becoming a better version of yourself to attract Mr. Right. You're aware of the importance of maintaining your identity, such as maintaining your own interests, hobbies, and friends throughout your relationship.

> **Remember, the most important opinion to a man is his queen's.**

If you diminish, shame, or demean him in public or private, it's like stabbing him in the heart with a knife. It cuts to the core. Let's recap the checklist of superhero deactivators and queen behaviors that attract the king.

SUPERHERO DEACTIVATORS

- The selfish *WIIFM* (What's In It For Me)? Syndrome. Operating in the mindset of my needs, my desires, my control, my victimhood, etc. Having the expectation for him to meet all your needs instead of how you can serve each other's heart attitudes.

o Criticizing, correcting, or redoing a man's work. The perfection syndrome is where there's consistent fault finding. He can't win, no matter what he says or does.

o Publicly or privately shaming your man for mistakes or shortcomings.

o Directing, instructing, or correcting a man on what he should do, how to do it, what to wear, and what he needs to change.

o Allowing your world to mesh into his. Being needy, insecure, jealous, and reliant on him to meet your needs.

o Not receiving a compliment. Rejecting him by negating his compliment, gift, or act of kindness. Reverse-training him to mistreat you and not give you compliments or gifts.

o Consistently talking about yourself or interrupting him. Not validating his feelings or ideas.

o Choosing man-projects to control and manipulate as a substitute for deeper feelings of insecurity or lack of self-worth. Acting like his mother.

o Unhealthy competition, "I'm better and can beat you" attitude. Being unwilling to apologize and constant one-upping. Always have to be right or have the last word.

o Drawing the man into your world of chaos and drama. Unloading on him with verbal diarrhea.

o Playing the victim and not taking responsibility for your words, actions, and choices. Ignoring how your words, attitudes, and actions are making him feel.

o Confronting him in an accusatory and snarky tone. Assuming the worst.

o Operating in the Yes Syndrome, losing yourself and allowing his world to become your world.

QUEENLY BEHAVIORS THAT ATTRACT THE GOOD KING

- ♥ Accept and believe an honest compliment with a simple thank you and smile.

- ♥ Ask about his dreams, goals, and interests. Listen and validate what he said. Affirm and invite him to tell you more.

- ♥ Intentionally look for things you can complement. If you aren't dating, practice with the man at the cash register where you shop. Notice something like his watch, smile, customer service, etc., and comment on it.

- ♥ Create a safe space where he feels comfortable expressing his emotions without fear of judgment, shame, dismissal, or belittlement.

- ♥ Thank him for any acts of thoughtfulness. Become aware when he does this and thank him with a smile.

- ♥ Speak complimentary things about him in public and one-on-one. i.e., "You look handsome in that color" or "You did a great job with___."

- ♥ Don't *tell* him what to do. *Ask* if you can make a suggestion. If he says "No," then honor that.

- ♥ Allow him to open the door for you, pull out your chair, carry something, let him help you or do things for you, and say thank you.

- ♥ When confronting him, assume he didn't realize what he did, no matter how stupid you think it is. Don't speak in an accusatory or snarky tone. Don't start with the words "You did" or "You are." **Instead,** say, "I know it wasn't intentional," or "You may not have realized," or "You may not be aware . . .."

- ♥ Don't redo his work or tell him how to do it *your* way. If he did the dishes, be impressed and thank him. Tell him that's sexy. He'll be encouraged to do more.

- ♥ Refrain from being his advice coach and telling him what he needs to change.

♥ Remind him often of his good qualities. Affirm his efforts to please you. Remember, a good man wants to be your superhero.

My marriage is guided by the core principles I've shared with you, and I apply them every day. They have allowed me to have a thriving and life-giving partnership with my husband, David. If we copy what successful people do, we will be successful.

Now, let's affirm you! I'm so excited about your journey of becoming a more healed version of you. You are very courageous and strong! Did you know the definition of a princess is one who is strong and courageous and takes dominion? By that definition, you are a princess of the King of heaven.

Taking action takes courage. You have done this by reading this book and doing the homework. Good practice makes good results. Bad practice makes bad results. As you apply the principles in this book, you are on your way to great new romance results. You are walking into a destiny of success to attract your Mr. Right.

Now, I encourage you to discover the beauty within yourself. Allow your inner radiance to emerge. We touched on some of the deeper emotional roots that drive our superhero deactivator behaviors. More often than not, they're rooted in past hurts, trauma, rejection, abandonment, betrayal, poor choices, and mistakes. Now you can forgive yourself, forgive the one(s) who hurt you, and walk in grace, love, and compassion for yourself.

The core foundation of most negative feelings is our inner identity. Learning to honor and accept yourself for the wonderful woman you were created to be will change the direction of your choices.

Remember, you are beautiful inside and out, gifted, smart, funny, generous, loved, honored, and cherished. As you come into these truths more and more, the old lies and mindset will drop off.

Learning new skills takes practice. As you continue to practice the exercises in this book and go over the principles, you are now changing your mindset to attract different results in your life. These revelations have put you in a position to attract a man who will love and honor you. They have also positioned you to maintain a strong, healthy relationship when he comes along.

I have a new book coming out that will walk you through a journey of healing in your identity from sexual abuse, trauma, etc. In my second book, I share my encounter in heaven that caused a complete shift in my inner identity. It will be a deep dive into inner healing, also incorporating the solfeggio healing frequencies of the music I write. Find more information on my website, JoannaHairabedian.com.

Beautiful princess, I'm SO PROUD of you! Now you're in a better mindset position to attract Mr. Right and experience wonderful romance results.

CONCLUDING WITH TWO VITAL HOMEWORK ASSIGNMENTS:

♥   I want you to take this moment to write down the qualities and characteristics of the man of your dreams. If you want to attract Mr. Right, this is vital. Here's an example of what my list was. Yours will be different.

> *"My husband loves me like no one has ever loved me. He is the man of my dreams who will be my life partner. He loves to travel and change the world with me. He is a mighty man of God, Holy Spirit filled, with utmost integrity and honesty, and is completely trustworthy in every way. He has no addiction issues of any kind. He either has worked through them and been completely delivered for years prior to meeting me or didn't have them to begin with.*
>
> *My husband is funny, energetic, kindhearted, generous, and brilliantly smart. He knows how to adjust my back with chiropractic adjustments. We make each other laugh. He is open-minded and coachable. He loves and celebrates the gifts within me, as I do the same for him. His family loves and accepts me. We are the perfect match.*

Did I get everything on this list and more? YESSS! Did I now have the skills (everything listed in this book) to nurture and grow our relationship when I met him? YESSS!

♥ Regardless of what your brain or emotions tell you, I want you to declare your declaration with unwavering emotion every single day. This, too, is vital. You can do this for ANY situation in your life!

If you don't do this, you may come into an accidental agreement with the opposite of what you want. **You must retrain your brain to expect what you are declaring.**

This is what I started doing every day with energy and emotion. There were many days that I didn't want to say it because my feelings were the opposite, but I did it anyway. **If I did it, you can do it!**

Now you are armed and equipped to make changes in your life and experience new romance results and wonderful things in your journey! I release love, light, and healing into your life. I'll leave you with my personal motto and remember: The BEST is yet to come for you.

Big hugs from me to you and God bless you!

L⁷ MANIFESTO

Learn. . . to receive from others.

Light. . . up the world with your smile.

Love. . .yourself.

Laugh. . . to heal your soul.

Leap. . . out of your fears.

Let. . . him be your superhero.

Launch. . . into your destiny now!

JOANNA HAIRABEDIAN

EPILOGUE
A Word from "Mr. Right"

Joanna is also writing a book for men, and I jokingly suggested it should be titled *7,000 Mistakes Men Make That Repel Good Women.* All kidding aside, I don't think women realize that men are looking for their perfect mate, just like women are. Instead of acknowledging their need for a life partner, men are often distracted with work, career, sports, etc. I was that guy who was disconnected from his inner needs, which had been replaced with my career. Until I met Joanna.

As a Type A personality who always seems to have an answer, I was rendered speechless one day by Joanna's question. She asked me what I like to do for fun. Dumbfounded, I didn't know what to say. No one had ever asked me that question. At that moment, it hit me that I was just doing life alone and not living it.

Joanna has drawn out parts of me that have learned how to have fun, laugh, and enjoy life. This is my first marriage, and after being single for a long time, I could never have imagined how wonderful our marriage could be. I know my heart is safe in Joanna's hands and hers in mine. Ultimately, I was looking for my queen and we would change the world together, which I have found and we are doing.

There's something about finding a true partnership that accelerates things. This is truly what's happened to me in being married to Joanna. King Solomon said:

> *He who finds a wife finds a good thing and obtains favor from the LORD.*
>
> PROVERBS 18:22 NKJV

I love that Joanna has become the missing wind beneath my wings, and I am hers! She is my perfect puzzle piece match, and we do everything together. She lives every bit of what she teaches others. I love you, Joanna!

The best is yet to come!

Dr. David Hairabedian

ABOUT THE AUTHOR

Joanna Hairabedian is widely recognized for her unique gift of helping women discover their rare inner gem that she calls "the Diamond Within." Each woman has unique facets on the inside that, when tapped into, cause them to "sparkle" and "shine." As a composer, vocal artist, and three-time national pageant titleholder, Joanna utilizes her platform to help women shine like diamonds. Whether it's gracing the cover of *TIARA* Magazine or learning from her own mistakes, Joanna understands the importance of a healthy mindset for success in love and life.

She has an online coaching program and conducts seminars around the country called Women of Royalty™, *Reveal the Diamond Within*®. These events inspire and empower women to discover their inner jewels and better fulfill their callings in life.

Joanna and her husband, Dr. David Hairabedian, found their *happily ever after* and married in 2014. They have a beautiful marriage and host an online spiritually-equipping platform called **VirtualChurchMedia.com**. Together, they have impacted millions of lives around the world.

FOR MORE INFORMATION:

https://linktr.ee/realanswers

CONTACT:

Info@virtualchuchmedia.com

Appendix A
SPIRITUAL HEALING
PRAYER

> *He heals the brokenhearted and heals up their wounds.*
> PSALM 147:3 NKJV

Heavenly Father, Your precious daughter and I come before the throne of heaven right now. We stand before Your amazing grace and ask forgiveness for our sins, mistakes, poor choices, and any areas of compromise. We thank you, Heavenly Father, that Your Beloved Son died on the cross so that we can be cleansed in our souls of everything and healed in our bodies.

The Word says that you heal the brokenhearted and bind up our wounds. By the power of the Holy Spirit, in the name of your Precious Son, I release healing and strength in the heart, mind, body, soul, and spirit for Your daughter who is reading this!

I pray over YOU, daughter of the King of heaven, for the mighty hand of God to overshadow every situation in your life right now. I pray for the baptism of His love to fill your soul and heart like never before. I commission the angels of God to move on behalf of you and your family in Jesus' name. Psalm 91 says that He will command his angels to guard you! I pray for every crooked path in your life to be straightened out.

I pray for the old mirror of the way you see yourself to be replaced with Heaven's mirror. From this point forward, I pray that you will see yourself through the loving eyes of your heavenly Father. I break off the spirit of trauma and infirmity in your life and release the light, healing, and love of God to fill you now in Jesus' name.

Every lying spirit and thing that torments or haunts you at night is broken off. My prayer is for peace to overcome that torment. I pray that any toxic people in your life will be removed and replaced with new people God has assigned to help you. I commission the Angels of God to do a spiritual housecleaning in your house and family. Psalm 91 says that you will rest in the Shadow of the Almighty and under His wings you'll find refuge.

Daughter of the King of Heaven, I bless you today with peace, with joy, with prosperity, with love, with healing, with wholeness, with health and a new mirror to see yourself as God sees you. I bless your coming in and going out. AMEN.

Are you aware of a special invitation to a heavenly banquet? Read on.

A SPECIAL INVITATION

> *And the prayer of faith shall save the sick, and the Lord shall raise him up; and if he has committed sins, they shall be forgiven him. Confess your faults one to another, and pray one for another, that ye may be healed. The effectual fervent prayer of a righteous man availeth much.*
>
> JAMES 5:15-17 KJV

Did you know that everyone has a special invitation to a beautiful banquet in heaven? However, just like any gala, we have to RSVP for this incredible event. Would you like to RSVP? Do you need a new identity? You can be born again as a new person in Christ.

Here's how you do it: Invite Jesus into your heart and ask Him for a personal relationship. He's been waiting for you. Ask Him to forgive all your sins and fill you with His Holy Spirit. No matter what you've done or what's been done to you, those things are washed away because of the precious Blood of Jesus that He shed on the cross. He was crucified on a cross for your sins so that you can be born again. When you acknowledge Jesus as your Lord and Savior, your life will change for eternity, and you can attend the beautiful banquet in heaven. He wants you to get to know Him and be in a relationship with Him.

PRAYER TO ACCEPT THE INVITATION TO HEAVEN

Jesus, I invite you into my heart for a personal relationship with me today. I confess all my mistakes and sins to you and ask for forgiveness. Change my heart, change my mindset, and baptize me in Your Holy Spirit. I choose to serve You. Fill my heart with a love, healing, and passion I've never known.

In Your name, I pray.

AMEN

Congratulations! Heaven is rejoicing with me right now!

If you need spiritual equipping, tools, teaching, etc. then please download this mobile app for **VirtualChurchMedia.com**. This app offers these great resources at no charge to you. It is sponsored by the donors and others who want to pay it forward. **Virtual Church Media** also features podcasts, TV broadcasts, healing music, and a one-year bible study. Learning the Bible is crucial because it serves as an amazing life guide.

VCM Mobile App

Made in the USA
Columbia, SC
13 March 2024

32716369R00089